I0159526

MARRIAGE FOR LIFE

BY
Pastor Louis Nettleton,
Lead Pastor of the Williams Road Free Will Baptist Church
in Columbus Ohio

Copyright 2016
By
Louis Nettleton

ISBN 978-1-940609-52-2 Soft cover

All rights reserved
No part of this book may be reproduced or transmitted in any
form or by any means, electronic or mechanical, including
photocopying, recording, or by any information storage and
retrieval system, without permission in writing from the copyright
owner.

Bible verses are from the CEV

This book was printed in the United States of America.

To order additional copies of this book contact:

Louis Nettleton
1100 Williams Road
Columbus, Ohio 43207
Or
www.amazon.com

FWB

FWB Publications
Columbus, Ohio 43207

BEING LIGHT, GIVING LOVE

FORWARD

It is a great privilege to write this foreword for Louis Nettleton who is a great asset to the body of Christ and dear friend to us. Marriage for Life is a relevant resource that does not compromise true biblical principles. Pastor Louis has created a true guide for couples who are seeking to prepare, to strengthen or to save their marriages. Louis has been consistent in his extreme passion for marriages to succeed. He is not just writing about marriage, but he has years of solid pastoral counseling experience that can now benefit so many others. He and his wife, Freda, have spent countless hours laboring alongside couples as they grapple with the hard things that seem to be against marital success. These hard things include infidelity, unhealthy attitudes and blended families. His lived experiences and training have equipped him for this amazing task to bring more God awareness in a practical way that will help couples to make needed relational changes. He has an amazing integrated experience of helping families, couples and individuals through difficult situations.

In our current society, marriage is not as respected for many different reasons. Many of us adults and this generation of Millennials grew up in homes adversely impacted by divorce, abuse and neglect. Our parents did the best they can do. As a result, play it safe and we build walls to protect us even from those closest to us. Many marriages never reach their greatest potential because they are entered into with the idea that "I will just divorce if he or she does not change." The beauty of this Marriage for Life book is that is encourages God as the Redeemer in every situation. When we allow space for God in our marriages, we began to receive God grace and to give more grace to our spouses.

As Counselors and Pastors, we appreciate his knowledge base and are eager to utilize this book in our ministry. This is a resource for couples at any stage of their marriage life. Marriage for Life encourages team work within marriages that is founded in healthy prayer life together. This book celebrates honor and grace in delivered in a way that encourages understanding. The stories of real individual offer hope to couples who may believe that their struggles are too difficult to repair. It is easy to identify with the testimonies of real people with real problems who are thriving today in their marriages.

God is willing to help if we yield to him and to each other. Broken attachments from childhood or early life experiences often make it difficult to attach to your spouse in healthy ways. Louis captures the pulse of God's heart for relationships to repair those breaches In Lesson Four, The Art of Partnership, it states "maintaining unity is accomplished from within defeating anger and releasing love, love that touches the heart of your spouse allowing peace to take control of your mess. How often do we forget that God is right there with us in our marriages? Don't be like the majority ignoring the power available to maintain the strength and unity of your marriage."

Marriage for Life explores the negative consequences of violating marital boundaries that are sure to compromise the safety of this sacred institution. This resource will sure to be a great tool in your relationship toolbox. It is good teaching at its best, complete, but accessible. Most in important, it is God's heart for our nation despite the trends to redefine or to minimize the role of God ordained marriages. Pastors and Small Group Leaders, utilize this book in small and large groups alike. This book can also be readily used in pastoral counseling and pre-marital sessions. Our prayer for those who read this book is for the Holy Spirit to be present and to personally confirm that anything in the Master's hands will prosper.

--Pastor Gwynmar Fraser and Pastor Yolanda Fraser

ACKNOWLEDGEMENTS

This book was not one man's efforts but a work of many. I wish to acknowledge all the contributors to this work. In my life the most important acknowledgement goes to my best friend Freda Nettleton. She is so much more than a wife she is my companion, mentor, and source of inspiration popping up at every corner, at every hurdle, and at every struggle lifting me up. Without her this work would not be complete. Her love is immeasurable, I love sweetheart.

The originators of the ideal for "Marriage for Life," Robert and Kim O'Quin have counseled scores of couples in their living room applying Biblical standards to the hearts of troubled marriages. Their testimony is overwhelming. In fact you will find their story inside this work and believe me their story is compelling and full of grace. What a beautiful couple. What a glorious picture of saving grace!! Thank you! Robert and Kim for your friendship, each of you have truly been a blessing.

David and Rebekah Ford are the "Marriage for Life" leaders at the Williams Road Free Will Baptist Church and they are doing a wonderful work for the Kingdom of God. Prior to their salvation both were divorced and met, each carrying excessive baggage into a budding new relationship. They have endured addictions, abuse, and disorders only to emerge from their darkness, not only finding salvation, but maturing into powerful leaders within the Church. Thank you for your contribution to this work I thank God for your labor of love.

Next, I want to acknowledge Pastor James and Paula Blake for their faithful walk with God and loyal service alongside us here at Williams Road Free Will Baptist Church, helping Freda and I to lead the local body of WRFWBC into a deeper understanding of God's Word. They also are contributors to this work. They have been a constant support and encourager I thank God for both of them. With their faithful help coupled with the grace and power of God we all have been empowered to rise up meeting every challenge victorious, glory to God! I pray increased power and success over each of you helping you in the journey ahead.

A few years ago Freda and I were in a deep pit struggling to find our place and purpose in the work of God. Pastor Gwynmar and Yolanda Fraser who I meet at Church planting group in Fort Worth have been great encouragers and wonderful friends. Pastor Gwynmar reached out to and asked me to help him and Calvary Life Worship Center out of Connecticut. I agreed and began helping him and Calvary Life to plant a local body in Keller Texas. The time I invested in those early years was short but invaluable to our restoration.

Then there is Kent and Laura-Lee Booth! I remember the weekly worship and prayer nights in their living room. We would spend hours worshipping in song and prayer, speaking life into each other I will never forget those nights of grace and love so freely shared by Kent and Laura-Lee. I Thank God for their friendship and their willingness to serve and minister to our needy souls, each of you often refreshed us renewing our passion for the ministry. I pray wisdom and strength into each of you as you faithfully serve our Lord and Savior Jesus Christ.

Table of Contents

MARRIAGE: A WALK WITH GOD 15

PRAYER IS A JOINT PROJECT! 19

COVENANT: AN ETERNAL PROMISE 27

COVENANT PART TWO: INTIMACY 35

UNITY: THE ART OF PARTNERSHIP 43

MARRIAGE MIRRORS I 53

GUILT OR GRACE 63

Marriage Mirrors II 71

Robert and Kim's Story 79

IN LIKE MANNER 95

Marriage after Divorce? 101

Miracles Still Happen! 113

MARRIAGE FOR LIFE

MARRIAGE: A WALK WITH GOD
Introduction

"The Institution of Marriage is most blessed when both Man and Woman are married to Christ"

Proverbs 18:22, He who finds a wife finds a good thing and obtains favor from the Lord.

Malachi 2:13-16, and this second thing you do. You cover the Lord's altar with tears, with weeping and groaning because he no longer regards the offering or accepts it with favor from your hand. But you say, "Why does he not?" Because the Lord was witness between you and the wife of your youth, to whom you have been faithless, though she is your companion and your wife by covenant. Did he not make them one, with a portion of the Spirit in their union? And what was the one God seeking? Godly offspring! So guard yourselves in your spirit, and let none of you be faithless to the wife of your youth. "For the man who does not love his wife but divorces her, says the Lord, the God of Israel, covers his garment with violence, says the Lord of hosts. So guard yourselves in your spirit, and do not be faithless."

Marriage for life ministries has been reaching out for better than six years now and in the span of those six short years there has been a dramatic increase in failed marriages even within the Church. Earthly thinking has become more problematic usurping Heavenly authority. God's standard is not to be compromised nor is it okay to overlook Biblical Truth for convenience. God has called us to self-sacrifice, yielding ourselves to Divine principles not earthly pleasures. Let me put it another way, people enter the Church bound with earthly thinking ignoring Biblical principles. The Word of God tells us to forsake the old sinful nature of man, lifting our heads beyond the earthly standard seeing a higher calling setting our affections on heavenly things. Colossians 3, tells us to lift up our eyes and behold Jesus sitting at the right of the Father in Heaven meaning as Children of God we seek to fulfill the call of God in our lives. Yet as a whole the Church has not done a good job teaching or preaching the need for self-sacrifice or surrender.

In **Genesis 3:8 "During that day's cool evening breeze, they heard the sound of the LORD God walking in the garden."** Though this verse comes after sin had entered the Garden, the first portion of verse 8, indicates that God had established a daily habit of walking with Adam and Eve, leading me to believe that God intended every married couple to establish a daily walk with Him. Perhaps you think it strange that a book on marriage begins with God and not the union of one man and one woman, but here we are about to launch into what I consider the most important elements in preserving your marriage, Trusting God! Submission to Biblical principles is the single most important factor in all of your relationships, especially your marriage. The divorce rate has climbed over 50%, within the Church making it increasingly necessary to proclaim the urgent need to return to Godly lives and Godly marriages. As we institute a proper walk with God I will be encouraging both husbands and wives to submit to the Biblical structure of marriage enabling each of you to build stronger relationships with God and your spouse. The purpose of marriage is to glorify God, for the marriage relationship is but a reflection of our personal walk with God.

The most important element we have in building right relationships is rooted in our prayer life. In our personal life, Freda and I daily seek God's place in our marriage. We turn to God praying wisdom, discernment, and protection over each other. In our individual prayer we seek a deeper love for God that translates into a deeper love for each other, a deeper desire to have a more obedient walk with God that leads us to pour into each other more Biblical truth. This increases spiritual strength, increasing the power of love in our lives. With each passing year we find ourselves praying more and more, and just when you think it cannot get any better, God takes you to another level surprising you with His vast love.

PRAYER IS A JOINT PROJECT!
Lesson One

Have you forgotten the power of prayer? Have you just grown weary of praying, or have you grown too busy so busy in fact you cannot find a place to stop long enough to pray? It's not that you don't love each other. You simply have let this very important part of your life get crowded out by all the voices demanding your attention. I have found that my wife and family are worth fighting for, and the most effective weapon for this battle is prayer. Prayer is not just asking for things, but inviting God into your life, your struggles, and even your arguments. Maybe things like fear, embarrassment, or selfishness keep us from praying? No matter the reason, it is time to humble ourselves before our Savior and get in sync with His divine will. In my experience, prayer is like a key that unlocks the power of God. It's opening the windows of heaven letting the blessings of God pour out. It's reaching up to touch the heart of God drawing power and love into our lives. I shared with the "Marriage for Life," group this last Sunday night about my experience being in a covenant relationship not just a contractual agreement. Over the last 40+ plus years speaking to the growth of my love and commitment to Freda, has grown beyond my ability to understand. The depth of satisfaction, the breadth of my peace, and the loftiness of my hope can only be extolled as HEAVENLY. This did not simply evolve, but was worked at, cultivated, and prayed over for years. It was facing fires together and rescuing each other, and most importantly, "Never walking away from each other!" What we have today God has preserved. By God's grace both Freda and I promised each other to love each other and to remain in our covenant through good times, bad times, health or sickness, through prosperity or poverty, and to always keep God a part of our three strand cord making our marriage all the more difficult to break. Personally I feel the greatest bond I have to Freda is my promise to protect her and to lift her up in prayer daily. It is hard to turn your heart against someone you are praying over daily. Because of prayer indifference never had a chance!

In all my experience counseling couples most husbands and wives do not pray together, let alone commit to battle the attacks against their marriage as one in Christ. Listen, with every fiery dart thrown, with every selfish act, and with every ounce of pressure placed on the family, prayer becomes essential. Prayer will lead you to seek God and all HIS power enabling you persevere every hardship, not giving in to the selfish whispers of divorce, but seeking God's original intention for your marriage. When dealing with the enemy that wants to destroy your marriage you need a tangible ally much like that of Aaron who held up Moses' arms in Exodus 17, being married I have an ally who holds me up, picks me up, and prays me up to the throne of God. My ally keeps me in the battle. I thank God for giving me such a faithful ally. Who is your ally? Who is praying over you? Who is praying for your marriage?

I Peter 3:7, Likewise, husbands, live with your wives in an understanding way, showing honor to the woman as the weaker vessel, since they are heirs with you of the grace of life, so that your prayers may not be hindered.

Husbands are to live with their wives period! A man should never leave his wife stranded. Early in my marriage I had a hard time realizing that my thoughts and actions spoke volumes to my wife. I was selfish easily forgetting to meet the needs of my wife getting so busy with my own activity I would forget to pick her up from work leaving her stranded. I come to understand that my lack of concern left her feeling helpless and vulnerable striking fear within her. She felt unloved second rate... She was right! But thank God for His grace, I can now safely say, "Freda, I will never leave you stranded again." Even in the household of God, too many husbands are being seduced to leave their wives chasing after selfish desires never stopping to think how his selfish actions that damage your wife's self-worth. God's word is clear - Husband live with your wife! Do not go chasing after another love motivated by selfish thinking. God is not in favor of divorce and has clearly called us to live faithfully with our wives. Honor your wife with your love, your attention, always speak well of her letting others see your devotion. Husbands you are stronger than your wife, use your strength to protect her never allowing your power to cause harm. Men you have a responsibility to mutual prayer which is not possible unless there is mutual love and forbearance, nor can the husband's prayers be acceptable unless he treats his wife with compassion and respect. When a man honors his wife He will pray over her throughout the day making it much harder to ignore or grow indifferent towards her. Please remember that your voice raised in anger towards her not only robs her of dignity, but strikes fear in her heart pushing her farther and farther away. Then there is the problem of focus, so why are you so focused on things that do not matter? Even if they are important to you don't lose yourself in the destructive things of this world. Stay centered on who truly controls your future. Whatever or whoever holds your attention, holds power over you. Don't let people rob you of joy, peace, happiness or to lead you to ignore God. Don't let people diminish your worth! Stay focused on God and stop giving away your power. I think the best way to sum this up is to put it this way: Husbands stop being so selfish, demanding, and controlling and use your power to love honor, and respect your wife. Seek to be the husband God has called you to be being.....

Ephesians 4:29, Let no corrupting talk come out of your mouths, but only such as is good for building up, as fits the occasion, that it may give grace to those who hear.

When I pray for people, passion grows in their favor. God's love is so strong and overwhelming that when I pray it fills me and spills out onto those I am praying over. When I pray the love of God strips me of my selfishness leaving compassion in its place. This compassion grows within me feeding my love for Freda, molding and making me into the husband God has called me to be being. Without a constant connection to God I cannot stay connected to my wife. Being connected to Freda emotionally and spiritually gives me a mirror image of my relationship with God. What proceeds out of my mouth is but a reflection of what is in my heart, not just towards Freda, but towards God as well. When I speak death, evil, hatred, disgust, or condescension into my wife, I am also speaking it into God.

I put a great deal of pressure on the husband in this matter seeing that they are to be the spiritual head of the family. This does not mean the wives are exempt from praying over their husbands. Both of you need to faithfully practice and employ the power of prayer in your marriage. If you are not given to speaking life into each other don't expect change to come. This comes only by staying in the word of God diligently seeking God's strength to overcome the embarrassment, and fear of praying over your spouse. Just so there is no confusion when I speak of praying over your spouse I mean out loud in the presence of your mate. If you're ashamed to speak life into your spouse you are more than likely ashamed of God as well. Let me put it another way. Stop serving the fear of your flesh and stand in the power of God.

Colossian 1:9-11, For this reason, since the day we heard about you, we have not stopped praying for you and asking God to fill you with the knowledge of his will through all spiritual wisdom and understanding. 10 And we pray this in order that you may live a life worthy of the Lord and may please him in every way: bearing fruit in every good work, growing in the knowledge of God, 11 being strengthened with all power according to his glorious might so that you may have great endurance and patience, and joy.

If we are to pray this over our brother and sisters how much more important is this prayer for our families? Husbands, wives, we are mutually responsible for one another's spiritual growth and mutually responsible to lead our Children into the presence of God. Family was the first place of worship. As the

Church has an under-shepherd, so is the husband to his family. Both he and his wife take on the role of teaching, learning, and applying the word of God into their own lives as well as their children. The scripture above says without such teaching our lives do not live up to the standard set. Prayer leads to teaching, teaching leads us to spiritual wisdom, and then the application of God's word into our lives. When this teaching is not fulfilled in the home, we will lose our children to the world. The unbelief or departure of our children is not the fault of the Church, but the fault or failure of parents to pray over their children, to teach their children Godly principles at home. Parents ask yourselves this question, "When do I lead my family in devotions or prayer?" Life has become so fast paced we no longer sit down to family discussions, prayer times, let alone Bible studies. Everybody has a phone and all our attention is placed on it instead of the Bible. Some will declare the Bible on their phones, but the real question is how much time do you spend in the Word? Over the years parents have sought to blame the Church for a lack of programs for their children, yet we spend one to three hours a week in Church while our children live with us 168 hours a week. So where does the weight of responsibility lay? The Church structure is nothing more than a place to gather for encouragement and support of the Biblical function of family.

James 5:16, Therefore, confess your sins to one another and pray for one another, that you may be healed. The prayer of a righteous person has great power as it is working.

Families caught in this age of information have an overwhelming need to be transparent. Praying together makes us transparent. Studying the Bible exposes weakness and sin in our lives, which should focus us, as husbands and wives to seek prayer and strength from each other. I learned a long time ago to trust God to expose sin. When the family spends time studying the word of God, opportunity is given to the Holy Spirit to convict and expose sin in our children. Trust God to lead your children to be victorious over their sin, but never forget that God leads through you. When we ignore the parental responsibility to lead our children into the word of God, we are closing the door on the Holy Spirit. God has plans on us to encourage one another over condemning each other when sin is exposed in our lives. When we pray, love fills our hearts letting grace take the first and foremost position in all relationships. There is power for healing hurts, solving arguments, and correcting our selfish acts enabling us to live in the power of forgiveness. Freda and I have learned that the power of forgiveness is much more rewarding than being right.

COVENANT: AN ETERNAL PROMISE

Lesson Two

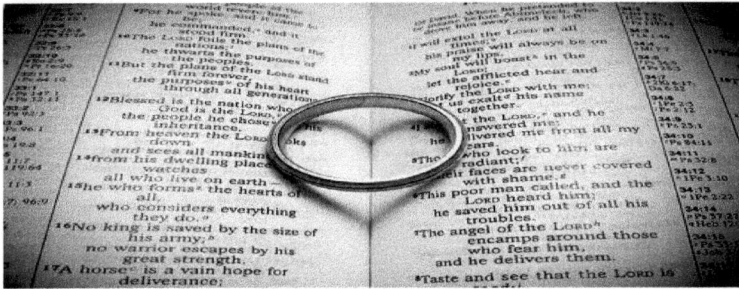

In 1950, 26% of all marriages ended in divorce and today over 50% of marriages end in divorce. It seems that we give more attention to our cell phone contracts than we do our marriage vows. Consider the current attitude or desire for instant gratification. It's no wonder people give up so easily on their marriages. Not many are given to working to preserve the divine structure of family. Listen, marriage is tough! Too many see their marriage as broken and instantly go looking for another mate based on all the failures of their current marriage. No matter the reason, God calls you to endure your hardships learning to be right with God in order to be your spouse's fit mate. Yet in their pursuit to make marriage work, the same problems keep popping up not having fixed the problem within. Let me make a suggestion - let God into your heart and mind helping you fix the problem within. The prospect of being seduced or losing interest in your spouse is diminished when you put God first. In fact it just makes being in love, being married, and raising a family that much easier. I know far too many people who just want to play Church. They go to Church for a very short season, but when life doesn't go the way they think it should they say things like, "This church thing doesn't work for me." This is the part that really gets me - they give up on God simply because they don't get their way. In order for God to bless you and elevate your life, you must die to self and come alive in Christ. You must sacrifice yourself, yielding every part of yourself letting God work providing what you stand in need of not demanding what you want. The same goes for marriage. Both man and woman must yield to each other for marriage to succeed stop being so selfish and let God do what needs to be done in life and marriage. I realize emotions are strong motivators in our lives and that love is an emotion but once a covenant (marriage) is established there are principles that should be preferred over emotional urges. We throw away the future blessings of God based on the present emotional stresses. There is too much wanting and not enough giving in marriages today. Even when you think you've done all the giving there are greater blessings for enduring, and upholding the importance of your marriage covenant! Your covenant relationship is patterned after God's covenant with mankind. Let me ask you a question, "Is it not true that you and I have frustrated the grace of God numerous times yet has not God no matter how mistreated, remains faithful?" The rhetorical answer is, YES! This leads us to the second step in getting in sync with God realizing the meaning and depth of vows or covenants of marriage.

Genesis 2:21-24, And the LORD God caused a deep sleep to fall upon Adam, and he slept : and he took one of his ribs, and closed up the flesh instead thereof; 22 And the rib, which the LORD God had taken from man, made he a woman, and brought her unto the man. 23 And Adam said

, This is now bone of my bones, and flesh of my flesh: she shall be called Woman, because she was taken out of Man. 24 Therefore shall a man leave his father and his mother, and shall cleave unto his wife: and they shall be one flesh.

In Genesis 2:18, God sees Adams need to have a companion, so HE create the animals of the earth allowing Adam to take dominion over them by naming each. But when all this is said and done, Adam still had a need for a more adequate companion. That brings us to the passage above where God creates women from Adam's rib and making it possible for them to fit together made Adam and Eve adequate mates. The very fact that God makes man to fit into woman speaks to how they complete each other, as well as how together they are to produce offspring. God goes even further creating a covenant marriage between man and woman stating this creation to be the design or structure as the precursor for civilizations, and that man would leave his father and mother and cleave to his wife. Jesus speaks in defense of the marriage covenant in Matthew 19:6, and Mark 10:9, saying, **"What therefore God has joined together, let not man separate."** When we look into the Word of God there is no confusion. God intends for one man and one woman to constitute a marriage, and that God's intention was for man to remain faithful to his wife, preserving the marriage covenant until death does part.

Every once in a while I have to stop and spout off without really thinking things through. I am saddened by the lack of concern so many, "so - called Christians," have towards biblical principles. I am really fed up with the selfishness of people who are more concerned about their fleshly desires rather than standing in obedience before God. I am equally concerned over people who compromise the Word of God for physical ease. Saying things like, "I can't afford to live alone or pay my bills." Have you forgotten, or not realized God first loved you and sent His only begotten Son to pay your sin penalty? You cannot proclaim to be a child of God and then choose to live in fornication (premarital consensual sex, casual sex, or simply living together) or adultery (a married man or woman engaging in sexual relations with someone other than your spouse). The beauty of one man and one women entering into a covenant relationship (marriage) represents the faithful and eternal relationship we are to have with God. In scripture God is pictured as the husband and we are his bride. The marriage covenant between a man and woman is meant to be a picture of God's commitment to His people putting a greater value on us showing each other grace, love, and forgiveness. We are to pursue our spouses as we would pursue God's salvation, one being a physical pursuit and the other a spiritual pursuit. God's promise/covenant with us says He will always be faithful to us and never forsake us. In the dictionary, covenant is defined as a binding agreement, written agreement usually under a seal. In the Bible, the teaching surrounding covenant is valued as a promise that should not be broken and if broken there are consequences. In Genesis 15, God declares a covenant to Abram and promises by this covenant the birth of a nation was to be birthed through Abram's seed. This promise made before Abram is still in effect and touches every born again believer to this very day. In verse 17, the scripture says a smoking furnace and a lamp passed between the carcasses prepared by Abram representing levels of importance not only to Abram but all believers throughout the course of history. The first level of meaning is that this promise encompasses heaven and hell, the furnace representing hell and the lamp the eternal glory of God. The second level of meaning rests in the pillar of smoke by day and the flame by night as the Children of Israel wondered in the wilderness. The final level of meaning is the mist or unclear image or the shadow of things to come in the Old Testament in contrast to the Light of understanding in the New Testament. God promised Abram a nation and that promise was not limited to the nation of Israel but to you and I being grafted into the Kingdom of God. God is faithful to keep His promise though his bride is unfaithful at times. God has given covenants, as eternal promises, depicting His power and commitment to love His bride (the Church, you and I).

Isaiah 41:10-13, Fear not, for I am with you; be not dismayed, for I am your God; I will strengthen you, I will help you, I will uphold you with my righteous right hand. Behold, all who are incensed against you shall be put to shame and confounded; those who strive against you shall be as nothing and shall perish. You shall seek those who contend with you, but you shall not find them; those who war against you shall be as nothing at all. For I, the Lord your God, hold your right hand; it is I who say to you, "Fear not, I am the one who helps you."

In like manner He calls us into the same covenant to be faithful to Him at all cost and in the same way faithful to each other in the marriage covenant. Stop looking at each other's shortcomings and realize you have the responsibility to love each other in spite of the shortcomings. I fear many churches have strayed away from the Biblical structure God intended for Church. The church's failure to teach proper Biblical structure especially the covenant relationship between the collective Church and God, has contributed to the decline in stable marriages within the Church. Marriage is meant to represent God's relationship with His people. When we accept Jesus Christ as our Savior, that relationship becomes a covenant relationship that finds God never moving from His position as husband to His bride (the Church). The act of salvation is to be seen as a marriage/covenant relationship one that proclaims God's faithful presence even when we fall short. The power of our covenant is not in the strength of the man or woman but in God, the third strand. What a marriage lacks in power and grace is supplied by the God, but He does not force His presence always waiting on our invitation. The beauty of God is that He never leaves us to fight the battles or struggles of our relationship alone, but is always there ready to step in to pick up our slack. Just as the pastor is the under-shepherd the husband becomes the under-husband. If your will look at II Corinthians 11, and the first four verses, they speak to this kind of relationship between God and mankind. **"I wish you would bear with me in a little foolishness. Do bear with me! 2. For I feel a divine jealousy for you, since I betrothed you to one husband, to present you as a pure virgin to Christ. 3. But I am afraid that as the serpent deceived Eve by his cunning, your thoughts will be led astray from a sincere and pure devotion to Christ. 4. For if someone comes and proclaims another Jesus than the one we proclaimed, or if you receive a different spirit from the one you received, or if you accept a different gospel from the one you accepted, you put up with it readily enough."** Then in Revelation 19:9, the Word speaks to the marriage between Jesus Christ and mankind, the Church being consummated with the "marriage supper of the lamb." If you're living in the worldly structure that values man's intellect, earthly beauty, physical strength, money or any other earthly power, it becomes increasingly difficult to find God let alone follow. When our vision is locked on fleshly desires, every part of our lives suffers but nothing suffers as much as our marriage. To find and follow God you must let the inner beauty of Biblical structure be expressed in our submission to one another, our faith towards God, and our commitment to the things of God thus allowing grace to rise within us building proper structure, aligning our lives to fit into God's order and form. Without proper understanding of God's structure we are unable to set Biblical priorities and values. At this point I wish to give a word to you, "Stop being so casual, so trivial, so divided in your walk with God! If you're going to please God it's time to step up your pace, ignite a singular focus, and stop fearing what the world will say. Don't wait! Make it today. It is your time to move from this world into presence of God! Now is the time to commit to God and each other. Don't let another week pass without rearranging your priorities into the Biblical structure called for in the Bible."

COVENANT PART TWO: INTIMACY
Lesson Three

Love your wife as Christ loved the Church

Intimacy is not limited to sexual behavior but should be integrated into every part of your relationship. The building of intimacy is accomplished by studying the object of your passion. Intimacy meaning, I see into you, I understand you, I know what you love and hate, I can finish your thoughts even as you complete mine, I pour into you the right portions, right words, and right emotions. The wife's intimacy finds her husband's silent comforting while the husband's intimacy finds his wives sharing of her emotions encouraging. You find the same structure being used in the Bible as the Word urges us to study to show ourselves approved unto God, so should be the study of our mates, to always be approving of each other. We learn in **Ephesians 5:22-33**, how God views the marriage covenant. He sees the covenant in the same arena as our marriage to Christ. We are called to keep the covenant of faithfulness just as we are to be faithful to God. Intimacy with God is reflected in the intimacy of marriage this covenant allows us to see more clearly the heart of God. Have you ever gone to an art museum? I have and viewed the collection by Renoir. The detail of his paintings requires a great deal of time gazing at the painting in order to take in all the fine details. In the same way we must spend time gazing into the Word of God to fine the deeper understanding that allows us to see the order and structure of the Bible. In this order and structure we understand what God has done, or is doing, and will do in our Churches, our lives, and our families. It tells us that God's covenant is a love that will not forsake us or leave us. When we understand this principle our relationship with church and family take on a much deeper meaning. In the same way husbands you need to gaze into your wife studying her in every way. There is no other way to build intimacy with each other. Stop being satisfied with sexual intimacy. Strive to connect on a deeper level. Will it take sacrifice - YES! Will it be easy - NO! But it will bring lasting strength to weather any storm you and your wife may face.

Ephesians 5:25, "Husbands, love your wives, as Christ loved the church and gave himself up for her..."

John Gills Exposition of the Bible says it this way, **"in showing respect, and doing honor to them; in seeking their contentment, satisfaction, and pleasure; in a quiet, constant, and comfortable dwelling with them; in providing all things necessary for them; in protecting them from all injuries and abuses; in concealing their faults, and covering their infirmities; in entertaining the best opinion of their persons and actions; and in endeavoring to promote their spiritual good and welfare: this love ought to be hearty and sincere, and not feigned and selfish; it should be shown in private, as well as in public: it should be chaste and single, constant and perpetual; it should exceed that which is bore to** neighbors, or even to parents, and should be equal to that a man bears to himself; though not so as to hinder, and break in upon love to God and Christ: many are the reasons why husbands should love their wives; they are given to be helps unto them; they are companions of them; they are wives of covenant; they are their own wives, yea, their own bodies, their own flesh, nay, as themselves; they are their image and their glory; and especially the example of Christ, in his love to his church and people, should engage to it."

Wow! Suddenly I feel convicted! What a list of things men ought to be toward or for their wives. No wonder marriages are falling apart. Who has taught men how to be covenant husbands? Look at this, In **Ephesians 5:2** it says, **"And walk in love, as Christ loved us and gave himself up for us, a fragrant offering and sacrifice to God."** Meaning, Christ gave away His time, service, and strength. He laid aside His own interest His own fame and even reputation that He might provide for His Bride, meaning the Church. He gave up everything even His own life to reconcile us to God. In essence Christ sacrificed (surrendered) for the sake of His Bride. Now stop just a moment and think of all the times you have fallen short, taking God for granted chasing after the pleasures of this world much like a scorned lover chases after another lover, yet He remains faithful to you! Note God is always ready to forgive giving you opportunity after opportunity to return to His grace. Wow! What a beautiful picture of God's covenant to each believer. God is urging each of us to commit, to the best of our abilities, to be faithful to the covenant promise we have made with our spouses. When driven by our fleshly desire our minds are closed to spiritual thought putting our marriages in jeopardy. But when we seek to fulfill the call of God to uphold spiritual purity our covenant relationship is preserved.

II Peter 3:9, The Lord is not slow concerning his promise, as some regard slowness, but is being patient toward you, because he does not wish for any to perish but for all to come to repentance.

The promise of God is an expression in which He shows importance of the object or function promised. In the case of marriage we need to realize that the family is the foundation for the structure later to be called the Church. In fact, marriage (your marriage) is a mirror reflection of your relationship with God. Listen! This makes marriage a valuable structure to be cherished not to be changed into the image of man, nor to be seen as just a piece of paper or something easily throw aside. When God makes a promise, it stands the test of time. You can always count on god keeping His word! God wants to see that the promise/covenant is meant to endure hardships, infidelity, selfishness, poverty, even sickness. If the Church would learn to give grace in the mirror image as God does to you and I, the world would be turned upside down. Grace would prevail touching people around the world leading each to understand the power of God's structure over mankind's desires. Satan understands the value of the marriage covenant. This is why he is attacking the family structure and marriage with such fervor.

Habakkuk 2:3, for the revelation awaits an appointed time; it speaks of the end and will not prove false. Though it linger, wait for it; it will certainly come and will not delay.

God is calling each of us to follow the Biblical pattern for marriage. In so doing marriages can be turned from destruction to restoration; the act of being reconciled into the joy of the Lord, the strength of our Lord, and the love of our Lord bringing peace and wholeness to our marriages. There are two problems with this, whether or not you're willing to surrender letting God lead you into the Biblical structure for marriage, or if you're willing to wait for your mate to arrive at the same place. Each of these essential qualities must be seen as investments in the future of your marriage. **Psalm 119:133, "Keep steady my steps according to your promise, and let no iniquity get dominion over me."** Don't give up! So many couples battle through hardships only to give up just before the victory is won. Don't be one of those couples that will get frustrated at the eleventh hour. The investment in God and in your marriage will outweigh your struggle. Let God give you the victory in His timing, not yours.

2 Corinthians 9:6, "The point is this: whoever sows sparingly will also reap sparingly, and whoever sows bountifully will also reap bountifully." You want to talk about investments God called Hosea to marry a whore named Gomer and after a year or so she leaves him for her past lovers. Hosea put a hedge about her. He invested in her and won her back in the end, buying back what was already his... What a beautiful picture of how God's love does not stop when we fall back into the arms of this world. His investment on the cross is always seeking to restore us to full fellowship. God wants you to invest in your marriage the same way Hosea invested in his. **Hosea 2:8, "And she did not know that it was I who**

gave her the grain, the wine, and the oil, and who lavished on her silver and gold, which they used for Baal."

Ezekiel 33:11, Say to them, 'As surely as I live, declares the Sovereign LORD, I take no pleasure in the death of the wicked, but rather that they turn from their ways and live. Turn! Turn from your evil ways! Why will you die, people of Israel?'

Rarely does God take you from the clutches of Egypt straight into the promise land! The journey is just too important to skip. There are lessons to be learned in the process of trusting God. If your marriage is in trouble there needs to be a turning from destruction to restoration, from accusations to forgiveness, from outward perspective to an inward perspective. Listen! What you focus on is the key to success or failure. Focus is not hard. What you focus on, well that is a different story. Some people say, "I can't sit still in church," but can go to a ball game sit for better than two hours. It is all about focus. How willing you are to sacrifice for Godly things? Are you willing to sacrifice for the restoration of your marriage? A better life awaits those who look within seeking to first make changes within themselves and trusting God to make the necessary changes in their mate. I am tired of trusting in the things of this world. I am tired of letting my selfish desires come between me and the love of my life. I am tired of trying to answer my own prayers or expecting God to do it my way. It is time to surrender into the love and care of my Savior letting him mold and make into HIS purpose. It's time to walk closer to God, not according to the flesh but according to the principles set forth in God's word. So, are you tried of walking in fear, failure, frustration, or in the poverty of power? The Word of God and the advice of Godly people can help you find the purpose, the principles, and the power to save or build a lasting marriage. **Proverbs 3:5-6, "Trust in the Lord with all your heart, and do not lean on your own understanding. In all your ways acknowledge him, and he will make straight your paths." Seek to agree, in your agreements the spark of love remaining in you will be kindled to a flame. Amos 3:3, "Do two walk together, unless they have agreed to meet?"**

UNITY: THE ART OF PARTNERSHIP
Lesson Four

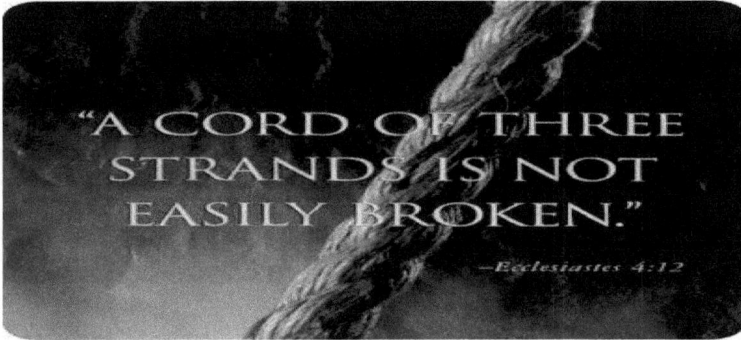

"A CORD OF THREE STRANDS IS NOT EASILY BROKEN."
—*Ecclesiastes 4:12*

Ecclesiastes 4:12, and though a man might prevail against one who is alone, two will withstand him—a threefold cord is not quickly broken.

In Ephesians 4, we see a strong exhortation for the Church to live in unity. In fact the process of spiritual growth and function of the Church is dependent on the body living in unity. When the Church learns to let the divine love flow, God releases power supplying the needs of every person in the body creating growth of the body. Since the Church is patterned on the structure of marriage, it only right for us to conclude that such unity is critical for the proper function of marriage. **Genesis 2:24, "Therefore a man shall leave his father and his mother and hold fast to his wife, and they shall become one flesh."**

You cannot be "one flesh," without living in unity. The marvelous thing about God's call to unity is that He does not expect us to do this by ourselves He is more than willing to wrap Himself about the husband and wife creating a three stranded cord that is not easily broken. Maintaining unity is accomplished from within defeating anger and releasing love, love that touches the heart of your spouse allowing peace to take control of your mess. How often do we forget that God is right there with us in our marriages? Don't be like the majority ignoring the power available to maintain the strength and unity of your marriage. I understand that it's all too easy to point fingers at each other slinging accusations justified or not. Looking to your spouse to solve the marital impasse only intensifies the impasse! This is where the presence of God pays off on the investment that has been paid into your marriage. If, and again I say, If you allow God to work in your marriage He will bring grace and peace into each of your hearts, but in order for this to happen each person must be willing to surrender the hurt and anger. Deep down you know that peace and harmony comes after you surrender to God's will. There's an abundant harvest waiting to be reaped, but so few are willing to pay the price for such a harvest... the sacrifice of self.

I have grown increasingly concerned over marriages unwilling to compromise for one reason or another, each contending party steadfast and unwilling to give an inch, each feeling entitled to more without giving more. Young men feeling trapped needing to get away for personal time with his friend or hobbies and the young woman left feeling neglected and longing for personal time with their husbands to fulfill their emotional needs, and with children these feelings only intensify. How sad to see so many husbands and wives unwilling to find common ground moving quickly into divorce thinking they have found an escape from their sadness. Today with divorce being so popular, too many young women proclaim that every relationship ends in arguments. Then she ask this question, "Is there any hope for me? Will I ever find the right man?"

Outside of finding Jesus as your Savior, there is nothing as important as finding the right person to share your life with under the structure formulated in the Bible. The most important part of the structure is not one man and one woman (though important,) not giving birth and raising children (though important,) but making God the third strand of your marriage. When a man and a woman are joined together in marriage under the Biblical structure their marriage is united with God. He wraps Himself about their lives adding a third strand giving strength for the journey ahead of them. God becomes your go to resource. Prayer takes center stage in your marriage life, as well as your family life strengthening your tie to God your spouse and your children.

There is a beautiful picture given to us in **Ecclesiastes 4:7-11, "Again, I saw vanity under the sun: 8 one person who has no other, either son or brother, yet there is no end to all his toil, and his eyes are never satisfied with riches, so that he never asks, "For whom am I toiling and depriving myself of pleasure?" This also is vanity and an unhappy business. 9 Two are better than one, because they have a good reward for their toil. 10 For if they fall, one will lift up his fellow. But woe to him who is alone when he falls and has not another to lift him up! 11 again, if two lie together, they keep warm, but how can one keep warm alone? 12 And though a man might prevail against one** who is alone, two will withstand him--a threefold cord is not quickly broken."

Vs. 7, **Again, I saw vanity under the sun:**

- Life is difficult enough and living without purpose is not only harder, but leaves us frustrated and bored. Living without purpose is letting life just happen. It's an open door for Satan to distract us from the priorities of life with pettiness, and selfishness. This causes many to pursue fleshly pleasures, never finding fulfillment. Following the Bible standard set forth allows structure to enter into our lives leading us to invest righteousness into our spouses yielding a return of peace, forgiveness, and grace. Believe it or not, some Christians seek to solve their problems using earthly thinking. But earthly thinking leaves you empty and still groping about in the darkness of this world. When lost in the darkness of failed marriage, we need an eternal source of light, energy if you will to find our way to God letting Him mend the brokenness of our relationships.

Vs. 8, **one person who has no other, either son or brother, yet there is no end to all his toil, and his eyes are never satisfied with riches, so that he never asks, "For whom am I toiling and depriving myself of pleasure?" This also is vanity and an unhappy business.**

- When God gave Eve to Adam He meant for them to fulfill each other emotionally, physically, and spiritually. Both were made in the Image of God making them complimentary fitting together in every way, each providing what the other lacked, and each satisfying the needs of the other. Both depending the on the other to bear fruit according to God's plan. It is the distortion of this Godly principle that seeks to destroy the makeup of the biblical family. Today more than any other time in our history Satan has launched a two-prong attack against Biblical principles. One rooted in the humanistic philosophy seeking to eliminate the very foundation of faith, and the other is an outright attack upon the moral structure of family. This is so critical because it is in the structure of family that God intended for faith to be passed along. God has established a structure for all of creation to function and this is especially true in the in institution of marriage beginning in Genesis 1, and continuing throughout the Bible.

Vs. 9, two are better than one, because they have a good reward for their toil.

- Investing into one another is critical in a lasting relationship. Freda and I early in our marriage did not realize the importance of pouring into each, praying over each other, or investing time into each while our children were young. This failure leads to many arguments and fights over money, feelings of neglect, or power struggles. There was a much deeper cause for the often erratic outburst letting life drive us into our own private worlds resulting in failure to invest time and attention into our love. While I loved my children, my love for them should not have outweighed my love for my wife, or her love for me. Husband and wives are teams that must work in unity and harmony to fulfill their function to bear fruit both physically and spiritually. Never lose sight of your spouse, for one day your children will grow up and move on, and all you will have left is the investment you have made into each other.

Vs. 10, for if they fall, one will lift up his fellow. But woe to him who is alone when he falls and has not another to lift him up!

- When I invest in someone I am not willing to give up quickly when they stumble. I see so many couples giving up on their marriage without a fight even when children are involved giving no lasting thought to the harm divorce causes. When you invest more in self than you do in your spouse, it makes it easy to protect selfish interest walking away from what you thought was the love of your life... It's rather disheartening to realize just how selfish you can be..... We are created by God to help invest in each other. Sacrifice is an essential part of a relationship. Without willingness to sacrifice selfish desires all of your relationships will be dysfunctional and ultimately doomed.

Vs. 11, again, if two lie together, they keep warm, but how can one keep warm alone?

- Intimacy is vital to a marriage for our deepest needs are met in periods of intimacy. This is not localized to sexual behavior although it certainly is an important part of the relationship. Intimacy starts long before you enter the bedroom like praying over each other, just sitting and holding each other, learning to do things you don't like for the sake of your spouse. Husband, communication is a wonderful tool to build intimacy and security into your wife. If you're not good at it, do it anyway. This investment will pay overwhelming dividends. Sometimes the best communication requires no words, just a simple nod of the head and a strong arm wrapped about her.

- Wife, in the same way you may have to step out of your comfort zone to communicate a depth of intimacy that cannot be achieved in the bedroom. Learning to pray life over your husband is so needed, learning to participate in his interests show him you care about what he cares about. Then finally the Bible says do not refuse to meet each other's physical needs, meaning sex.

- **I Corinthians 7:5 "Don't refuse to meet each other's needs unless you both agree for a short period of time to devote yourselves to prayer. Then come back together again so that Satan might not tempt you because of your lack of self-control."**

- Letting your spouse go out into the World hunger for sex gives Satan all He needs to mount an attack seeking to destroy your marriage. Do not use sex as a vice to manipulate your spouse for personal desires.

The act of sex is a blessing given to enhance your love and attention towards each other. I also believe that the blessing of sex points us to spend more time in intimacy with God. There are such sweet blessing as we grow more intimate with God.

Vs. 12, **and though a man might prevail against one who is alone, two will withstand him--a threefold cord is not quickly broken.**

- Just as man needs a complimentary helper mankind stands in need of a spiritual influence to be complete. The Creator never meant for us to live life without fulfilling our spiritual purpose through Jesus Christ. God becomes the third strand of our marriage making all the harder to break. Make God first in your life! This requires you to take to diligently pursuing God in His word and praying over your spouse keeping Satan's fiery darts from finding their target.

Letting God take control makes all the difference in the world. There are too many people laboring in the misleading wisdom of this world and the divorce rate continues to climb even in the church. The only hope we have is to turn to the Word of God and follow the structure set forth within its pages then and only then can we find a way to maintain or save our marriages.

MARRIAGE MIRRORS I
Lesson Five

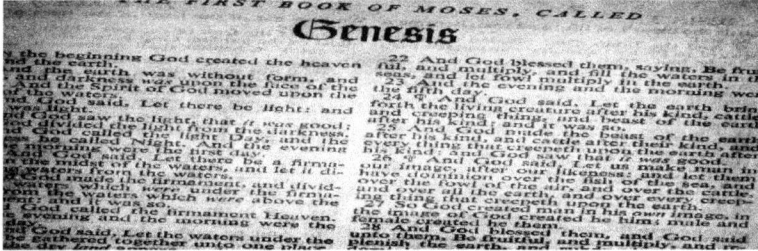

"There is Overwhelming Evidence of God's Structure"

Satan's attack on the family is evident and growing stronger with each new day. His plan has always been aimed at the family structure because He knows that in destroying the family structure He cripples the Church. Satan has been diligent and patiently planning and implementing his attacks at the very heart of God's creation and has no plans of letting up. It is through the family that the most effective attacks against the Church are leveled. His attacks on the family using the advantages gained in the sexual revolution over the last 50, or more years is bringing the Church to the verge of destruction. Satan has been changing minds, building strongholds, and leading individuals to think more highly of themselves than they should, resulting in the increased trust in physical or earthly wisdom, natural science elevating man to think himself god, and with humanism taking root proclaiming the "here and now" as all we have so let's party, and the worst of all is the entitlement mentality thinking that everything should come without a price. This thinking has emboldened people to stand out becoming more vocal than ever using the rise of heterosexual couples moving in with each other as the natural thing to do thus eliminating marriage. Gay rights redefining marriage all together has put pressure on the church to relax the Biblical standard. This speaks to the very core of truth and validity of God's Holy Word. For the man and woman of God, it is no longer good enough to focus inward protecting what we have. We must learn to let the Light of the God's Holy Word shine brightly upholding truth and making a way for souls to escape the darkness of this world. If we don't understand the importance of persevering in the Biblical structure of marriage and the importance of family, we have failed!

Created in God's image

Genesis 1:27, "So God created man in his own image, in the image of God he created him; male and female he created them."

- Here the scripture says both man and woman were created in the image of God, but there is a significant difference in the way they were formed from the rest of creation. Man being from the dirt and woman being form Adam's rib as well as the dirt, the most significant difference is God breathing into each a soul, each being in the image of God neither valued more important than the other. Being taken from Adam's rib signifies the need for emotional connects in a woman's life, while on the other hand man is more tasks-oriented. I am led to think the creation of Adam and Eve is not only the start of mankind, but their relationship is meant to be a reflection of our walk with God. I cannot help but think that the marriage relationship is a physical representation of how God desires to be united with mankind spiritually. As woman is fit for man and man fit for woman, together they show how every marriage and family needs God to fit completing His will. Man as the under-husband represents the presence of God, and woman taken from man was fit for man, would represent mankind. The institution of marriage reflects how God interacts with mankind. Even the formation of the Church is to be seen following the family structure in due time. Being created in the image of God, indicating a cognitive, emotional and spiritual development with these special qualities resting within they rest in the weakness of flesh! That weakness is due to sin and as a result of sin we all have to face death in this physical life, this more than anything speaks to our need for completion and only God can give the needed life in the face of our impending death. This physical death is a reflection of the coming spiritual death those without saving grace. Just as the call of God to the individual to receive saving grace through faith, **(Ephesians 2:8-9)** that same grace is used to empower every marriage to fulfill the will of God. We stand in need of God!

The First Marriage Covenant

Genesis 2:18, Then the LORD God said, "It is not good that the man should be alone; I will make him a helper fit for him."

- In the beginning man was alone and in need of companionship, the animals could not satisfy Adam on any level. This was not a process of discovery but a part of the God's plan. I believe by creating Adam first this affords him the right to take dominion over the animals establishing him as protector. Since the relationship with the animals did not completely meet his needs, God stepped to the next level of creation creating Adam a fit mate. This fit mate was much like Adam yet different molded by the hands of God so Adam could fit into woman. Woman could converse with Adam, nurture him, love, and embrace him making them fit companions thus establishing God's plan for marriage and ultimately the seed for the family unit. Without a fit mate to propagate he could not yield a harvest of glory unto God the Creator. God intended children to give glory to the parents as well as the Creator and to be raised to worship the Creator (father's influence) and nurtured (mother's influence) in the word of the Almighty.

- Not only do I see this as the beginnings of the family structure, but I see the seed for the beginnings of Church structure. I see in the family principles spilling over into the local Church. The strength of the family dictates the strength of the Church. To me Satan's attacks on the family make more sense seeing the family structure the precursor to the Church structure. Destroy the family, cripple the Church.

- Believers are not meant to stand alone, but within the corporate structure are meant to be lending strength to each other. Not even the corporate church is meant to stand alone but in union with a fit mate the Holy Spirit.

Genesis 2:20-24, "The man gave names to all livestock and to the birds of the heavens and to every beast of the field. But for Adam there was not found a helper fit for him. So the LORD God caused a deep sleep to fall upon the man, and while he slept took one of his ribs and closed up its place with flesh. Then the LORD God made a woman from the rib he had taken out of the man, and he brought her to the man. The man said, "This is now bone of my bones and flesh of my flesh; she shall be called 'woman, ' for she was taken out of man." For this reason a man will leave his father and mother and be united to his wife, and they will become one flesh."

- Adam naming each of the animals is a sign of authority over the animals with this act an order is being established, boundaries are being put into place. Every part of God's creation has a place and a function, not so much as in an order of importance but as in being complimentary. The Law of Complementarity says that the structure of the body allows performance of certain functions, the "Structure determines your function." This is exactly what God has done in His creation each part complimenting each other in form and function, each with the expressed ideal of yielding fruit and reflecting the nature of God in its function. If the relationship does not allow this type of form and function thus yielding fruit without artificial means it is not God's plan, but the selfish desires of the individuals.

- Adam not finding a fit mate amongst the animals teaches us the importance of our form and function which is critical to God's design. God had spoken every other part of creation into existence yet with man and woman He forms them with His hands first designing man then woman taking a rib from man so they would recognize their unique form and function together. The first institution created by God is family one man taking one woman in marriage and yielding fruit to bring glory and honor to God.

- In the structure of family, God is teaching us how to build a relationship not only with our spouse and family, but more importantly with Him. Man being the protector and provider reflects the imagery of God the Father while woman, the giver of life and nurturer, becomes the image of mankind. Mankind stands in need of God for new birth as woman stands in need of man for life to come forth showing, clearly the form and function of marriage and family.

- In this passage I also see a call to sacrifice old relationships and surrender to each other for marriage to work. In Marriage a new life begins but not before leaving behind your old life in your parents household. Then cleaving to your spouse in newness of life leaving the physical realm behind and cleaving to spiritual through Jesus Christ. The newness of life in Christ is reflected in our love for our spouses as in, loving God with all our heart, mind, and soul. (**Luke 10:27**)

- Marriage is consummated (becoming one flesh) with man fitting into woman, just as God fits into us and dwells inside mankind's heart or soul. At that point the Child of God becomes a temple of God, for upon salvation the Holy Spirit dwells within each believer. Our temples/bodies are to be kept clean and pure, for as we are committed or as the Apostle Paul states we are married to Jesus, we are meant to be faithful to our one true love, not giving ourselves away for selfish pleasure. Men, we are not to enter Godless temples for selfish pleasure for in doing so we are committing adultery against the Creator, nor should women allow their temples to be defiled with selfish pleasures. (**I Cor. 6:12-20**) God's structure is one man faithful to one woman joined in a holy covenant thus being faithful to each other just as we are to be faithful to God.

- Blood touching blood (sperm and egg) creates life the moment of coming together. New life is set in motion and fruit is produced! Seeing that God molded and sculpted man and woman by His hands making them not only fit mates but as temples to house the Holy Spirit stresses the importance of our sanctity, purity, oneness, and fidelity to God and spouse. The Blood of Christ touches our souls forgiving our sin creating the newness of spiritual life so in the reproductive form and function we see a physical reflection of new birth in Christ He becomes the husband in our spiritual walk and we are to produce spiritual fruit we are to be absolutely committed to Christ. **(Psalm 37)**

- In **John 3**, Jesus is talking to Nicodemus about the two births the child of God must go through one being physical and the other spiritual. It never ceases to amaze me at how the physical reflects the spiritual, if we would learn to see beyond ourselves there is a world of evidence pointing to the spiritual needs of mankind. For example water is involved in the birth of the Earth in Genesis one, it is used to symbolize the miscarriage of society and a fresh start in Genesis 6,7, and 8, here in John 3, the physical and spiritual are mixed to show the mirrored reflections of God's salvation the fruit of new life in Jesus. You could also make a cause for the Red Sea and the Children of God passing through the canal into the birth of a new nation, or the passing through the water of Jordan into the promise land.

- **Hebrews 5:13, everyone who lives on milk is not used to the word of righteousness, because they are babies. 14 But solid food is for the mature, whose senses are trained by practice to distinguish between good and evil."**

- In this passage our spiritual growth is symbolized in the growth of a baby into an adult. As a baby you must be nourished with milk, but you should desire meat as you grow. This passage uses physical food to illustrate how a new babe in Christ needs the milk of the word but should grow to desire meatier or deeper things of the Word of God. There is an immeasurable importance placed upon digging into the word of God not just for you daily life but in your family and in your marriage. Family is the basis for teaching children about Jesus, demonstrating divine love in our marriages so our children learn the importance of God's love in their lives, it's about sharing the love of God teaching children to see beyond themselves destroying the entitlement mentality making them servants not slaves. (**II Timothy 3:16-17**)

Sin in Marriage and its Consequences

Genesis 3:1-7, "Now the serpent was craftier than any other beast of the field that the LORD God had made. He said to the woman, "Did God actually say, 'You shall not eat of any tree in the garden'?" 2 And the woman said to the serpent, "We may eat of the fruit of the trees in the garden, 3. But God said, 'You shall not eat of the fruit of the tree that is in the midst of the garden, neither shall you touch it, lest you die.'" 4. But the serpent said to the woman, "You will not surely die, 5. For God knows that when you eat of it your eyes will be opened, and you will be like God, knowing good and evil." 6. So when the woman saw that the tree was good for food, and that it was a delight to the eyes, and that the tree was to be

desired to make one wise, she took of its fruit and ate, and she also gave some to her husband who was with her, and he ate. 7. Then the eyes of both were opened, and they knew that they were naked. And they sewed fig leaves together and made themselves loincloths."

- Remember the woman was taken and created from Adam's rib making her the perfect or fit mate for Adam. Adam had received the one law directly from God and he was responsible to teach Woman the law of God. This does not mean women cannot hear directly from God, but does speak to the order of the house or in this case the order of the Garden. Man is to be the leader of the family leading them deeper into the Word of God. He is also the protector of his family, to the best of his ability, not so much from physical harm, though indicated, but from the wiles of Satan and the attacks the world will launch against their faith. I see here the importance of family devotion, family prayer, husband and wives praying over each other preserving their families, in the grace and knowledge of Jesus Christ our Savior.

- Notice that Satan does not attack Adam, but woman wishing to take her out of God's order or position pitting the woman against man making her a lure to influence man into sin. Adam failed to protect woman as he should have stepping between Satan and woman meeting the tempter head on. But it was easier to stand off to the side letting this injustice occur right in front of him trapping both Adam and Woman in sin.

- Prior to the temptation of the serpent, Adam had not taken authority over woman... Perhaps God's design was for them to have the same authority. But God had given the law/commandment to Adam and trusted Adam to follow His command. This failure of Adam is seen in marriages across this land, it is seen in fatherless homes, and even with the father in the house far too many families are described as dysfunctional and I lay this failure on the shoulders of husbands and father who fail to follow God's structure. Without proper spiritual leadership the family structure is doomed to failure simply because too many fathers are standing off to the side watching and not leading.

- The serpent seeks out the newest member in the Garden, the one whom the law had been not been directly given, for Adam had received the law first hand from the Creator. You have to realize Satan wants to destroy your marriage and family by playing on your weakness, not your strength. This makes spiritual insight a must, spiritual truth essential to success, and spiritual power, your only hope of victory against the fiery darts of Satan. (**Gen. 2:16**)

- Satan's first attack was against God's covenant of marriage and took place in the home! I believe the structure of family is the precursor to corporate worship. Meaning your church is no stronger than the families of your corporate assembly. God intended the family and the Church to dwell in unity letting God becomes the third strand making it increasingly harder for Satan to disrupt our marriages let alone destroy our families. If Satan corrupts our families He then corrupts the Church then the Church loses its power of influence to lead people to believe in God. **(Ephesians 4 & 5)**

GUILT OR GRACE
Lesson Six

Genesis 3:8-13, And they heard the sound of the LORD God walking in the garden in the cool of the day, and the man and his wife hid themselves from the presence of the LORD God among the trees of the garden. 9 But the LORD God called to the man and said to him, "Where are you?" 10 And he said, "I heard the sound of you in the garden, and I was afraid, because I was naked, and I hid myself." 11 He said, "Who told you that you were naked? Have you eaten of the tree of which I commanded you not to eat?" 12 The man said, "The woman whom you gave to be with me, she gave me fruit of the tree, and I ate." 13 Then the LORD God said to the woman, "What is this that you have done?" The woman said, "The serpent deceived me, and I ate."

- When God arrived in the Garden, at the appointed time, Adam and woman were hiding from the presence of God as does so many couples even knowing they need God. God's plan is to be involved from the beginning of every marriage desiring to be the third strand. (**Eccl. 4:12**) Hiding from God never works out! All you have left are the consequences of your actions resulting in guilt rising within leading to self-justification. As we see in Adam and the woman's case, they sought to cover themselves with leaves hiding their nakedness before meeting God in the Garden. Notice that their attempt to cover themselves did not give them peace. Self-righteous plans are insufficient always leaving us soaking in the poison of guilt producing anger and confusion. I believe the fig leaves symbolize mankind's desire to justify, but I believe it is more important to see this as rebellion denying God's structure. God's plan from the very beginning was obedience to Godly structure, but when sin occurs God has a remedy through the shedding of innocent blood. Reconciliation is achieved by letting God confront your sin and seeking His forgiveness. It's the same with husbands and wives. Forgiveness cannot be reached without confession leaning on love finding forgiveness in grace.

- But grace (God) sought them out to expose their error. Reconciliation requires being exposed by the grace of God. It makes no sense to hide from God. Again Adam had a chance to stand and take his rightful position, but instead blames the woman then the woman blames the serpent. Husband and wives are always seeking to blame somebody else for their failures. The problem rests within and not in others... even when you're the victim the battle for restoration begins within. (**Psalm 51**)

Judgment

Genesis 3:14-23, The LORD God said to the serpent, "Because you have done this, cursed are you above all livestock and above all beasts of the field; on your belly you shall go, and dust you shall eat all the days of your life. 15 I will put enmity between you and the woman, and between your offspring and her offspring; he shall bruise your head, and you shall bruise his heel." 16 To the woman he said, "I will surely multiply your pain in childbearing; in pain you shall bring forth children. Your desire shall be for your husband, and he shall rule over you." 17 And to Adam he said, "Because you have listened to the voice of your wife and have eaten of the tree of which I commanded you, 'You shall not eat of it,' cursed is the ground because of you; in pain you shall eat of it all the days of your life; 18 thorns and thistles it shall bring forth for you; and you shall eat the plants of the field. 19 By the sweat of your face you shall eat bread, till you return to the ground, for out of it you were taken; for you are dust, and to dust you shall return." 20 The man called his wife's name Eve, because she was the mother of all living. 21 And the LORD God made for Adam and for his wife garments of skins and clothed them. 22 Then the LORD God said, "Behold, the man has become like one of us in knowing good and evil. Now, lest he reach out his hand and take also of the tree of life and eat, and live

forever--" 23 therefore the LORD God sent him out from the garden of Eden to work the ground from which he was taken.

- Judgment upon the serpent came in three phases:
  - o To slither around on its belly eating dust all its days.
  - o Putting enmity between it and the woman. (John Gill says, "Woman was delighted with the serpent, and laid it perhaps in her bosom/lap, adorned her neck with its windings, or made it a bracelet for her arms; and being a peculiar favorite, the devil made choice of it as his instrument to deceive her; but now being beguiled hereby, she conceived an antipathy against it, and which is become natural between the serpent and man...")
  - o The third is the most powerful judgment against the serpent and speaks to woman being elevated to a vessel of honor. **Genesis 3:15** is the first prophesy of the coming Messiah and the entry of the Messiah through woman. God seems to be saying, "You want to destroy my plan by corrupting marriage then it will be through the family structure a Savior will come birthed of woman and He will crush your head."

- Judgment upon the woman is also a three phase judgment:
  - Pain and sorrow in childbirth but out of her pain comes the greatest blessing of all the giver of life both physically and spiritually as she is the chosen vessel for the Messiah's entry into this world. (the pain is a constant reminder of sin's effect upon the earth)
  - The wife having been crafted from Adam's rib is now to desire a husband. The emotional sensessation rises within many women crying our for the protection of a man. We see so many women using their beauty to lure a man's attention, not waiting on God to provide a fit mate.
  - Husband shall rule over the wife, meaning she is to be in subjection to the Husbands will making her an encourager, mentor, and supporter of her protector.
  - Another interesting fact is that woman was created out of man and now subject to man as protector and providerto come the bibilical structure.

- Judgment upon man is also a threefold judgment;
  - Because he listened to the voice of his wife and not the voice of God the earth was now cursed and thorns and thistle grow easier than crops for food or beauty. (**Acts 4:19, "Whether it is right in the sight of God to listen to you rather than to God, you must judge..."**)

- o Interesting fact Adam was made from the dirt and is now subject to the curse upon the ground.
- o Work is made more difficult indicated but the sweat of his brow or face.
- o Death now rest upon Adam's shoulders. **(Romans 5:12, "Therefore, just as sin came into the world through one man, and death through sin, and so death spread to all men because all sinned...") (Rev. 22:14)**

- Adam Takes responsibility over Eve by giving her a name. Interesting fact Eve means, "Life." In Eve both physical and spiritual life rested. What an honor... Not to usurp her position over man or to manipulate him but to respect him for how he loves, honors, provides and protects her.

- God covers Adam and Eve's sin with the first sacrifice the shedding of blood for a sin covering. Sin requires the shedding of blood and here we see the structure put into place for the putting off of sin. The ultimate sacrifice was to be made through Jesus Christ. This is also critical in the case of Cain in that he failed to follow the structure of God which led to pride and rebellion. I believe Cain's offering was rejected for his rebellion against God's plan making his plan equal to God's, an act of defiance. **(Matthew 26:28, Hebrews 9:22)**

- Adam and Eve were expelled from the garden lest they be tempted to eat of the Tree of Life. The Tree of Life is now rooted in the Cross. The aspects of eternal life are meant for righteousness, not selfishness. Thus the whole of life is rooted in the man's need to rise to a standard of righteousness (**Matthew 5:6** & **6:33**) which within himself he is not capable. The tree is next symbolized in the Cross were Jesus becomes the ultimate sacrifice for the sins of mankind paying the price of man's sin and upon receiving the grace of God via faith the righteousness of Jesus the scripture then calls us to pursue the righteousness of Christ with all diligence. (**Galatians 6:1-10**)

Marriage Mirrors II
Lesson Seven

Isaiah 61:10, I delight greatly in the LORD; my soul rejoices in my God. For he has clothed me with garments of salvation and arrayed me in a robe of righteousness, as a bridegroom adorns his head like a priest, and as a bride adorns herself with her jewels.

Ephesians 4:1-16, I therefore, a prisoner for the Lord, urge you to walk in a manner worthy of the calling to which you have been called, 2 with all humility and gentleness, with patience, bearing with one another in love, 3 eager to maintain the unity of the Spirit in the bond

of peace. 4 There is one body and one Spirit--just as you were called to the one hope that belongs to your call-- 5 one Lord, one faith, one baptism, 6 one God and Father of all, who is over all and through all and in all. 7 But grace was given to each one of us according to the measure of Christ's gift. 8 Therefore it says, "When he ascended on high he led a host of captives, and he gave gifts to men." 9 (In saying, "He ascended," what does it mean but that he had also descended into the lower regions, the earth? 10 He who descended is the one who also ascended far above all the heavens, that he might fill all things.) 11 And he gave the apostles, the prophets, the evangelists, the shepherds and teachers, 12 to equip the saints for the work of ministry, for building up the body of Christ, 13 until we all attain to the unity of the faith and of the knowledge of the Son of God, to mature manhood, to the measure of the stature of the fullness of Christ, 14 so that we may no longer be children, tossed to and fro by the waves and carried about by every wind of doctrine, by human cunning, by craftiness in deceitful schemes. 15 Rather, speaking the truth in love, we are to grow up in every way into him who is the head, into Christ, 16 from whom the whole body, joined and held together by every joint with which it is equipped, when each part is working properly, makes the body grow so that it builds itself up in love.

Walking worthy in the structure of God's calling; Unity in the family structure is vital to a healthy family structure. In **I Timothy 3:4 "They (husbands) should manage their own household well—they should see that their children are obedient with complete respect,"**

The father is in charge of harmony within the family unit making sure unity is maintained for emotional and spiritual health. When you look at **Ephesians 6:1-9**, you notice an order or structure to the family with each member of the family having a place and function. When maintained produces unity. Without unity chaos ensues and the family loses sight of God, parenting from a place of ease instead of form and function. So many of our children have been raise out of parental ease leaving them undisciplined and self-absorbed.

Eph. 4:1-2, the meaning of forbearing one another is living in harmony in every part of our life. I believe love is best measured by our willingness to maintain unity/harmony in our homes and churches. Putting up with one another in harmony (unity) is the only way a family and church can function properly. Great importance is placed upon unity. We must learn the basis for heavenly blessings with each person staying in their place, laboring together in the love of God. The primary function of the under-shepherd is unity and the under husband primary responsible is unity/harmony in the family structure. Christ is the Shepherd and Husband of the Church. We are merely the under-shepherds and under-husbands respectively.

Ephesians 6:4 "Fathers, do not provoke your children to anger, but bring them up in the discipline and instruction of the Lord." Proverbs 3:6 "In all your ways acknowledge him, and he will make straight your paths."

The greatest need of the husband/father is to lead his wife and family into a proper attitude of seeking Christ, not relenting to personal ease. This kind of parenting, or thinking peace is based on personal comfort. An "out-of-sight out-of-mind," way of disciplining is improperly molding your child and letting children at any age live without boundaries. This does not build self-esteem, but chaos. Bring back the family time at the table, family devotion, and reestablish a family altar to help you find real peace under the form and structure of God's word.

Ephesians 4:7-16 speaks to the measure of grace Christ has placed into each believer. This is not just saving grace, but grace to live by or power to endure hardships, wisdom to help you solve the stressful times at home or at work. Seeking God in unity releases the grace of God into our marriages and home life empowering families to grow in love, respect and spiritual maturity. Grace is seen in God imparting gifts for the equipping (form and function) of the saints for the work of the Church as well as the work of the family. It is important to see this grace and power are not limited to the Church but is power and wisdom for every parent to maintain their marriage and family in the grace of God. Each believer or member of the family is to be learning his or her place in the Church and family. In so doing, they are led to maturity, learning and experiencing the truth of God's word allowing every member to grow fulfilling God design. **Ephesians 4:16**, our goal for both family and Church to grow yielding fruit! In the process of growth, we see several qualities given to us throughout scripture. The need is to work together in a unified direction, directing our combined attention to God not selfish pleasures, and living out life in the Church and home in obedience to Godly principles set forth in the Bible. Finally without a genuine love for God growth does not take place.

Ephesians 5:22-33, Wives, submit to your husbands as to the Lord, for the husband is the head of the wife as Christ is the head of the church, his body, of which he is the Savior. Now as the church submits to Christ, so also wives should submit to their husbands in everything. Husbands, love your wives, just as Christ loved the church and gave himself up for her to make her holy, cleansing her by the washing with water through the word, and to present her to himself as a radiant church, without stain or wrinkle or any other blemish, but holy and blameless. In this same way, husbands ought to love their wives as their own bodies. He who loves his wife loves himself. After all, no one ever hated his own body, but he feeds and cares for it, just as Christ does the church-- for we are members of his body. "For this reason a man will leave his father and mother and be united to his wife, and the two will become one flesh." This is a profound mystery-- but I am talking about Christ and the church. However, each one of you also must love his wife as he loves himself, and the wife must respect her husband.

Man in the marriage relationship should make his wife a priority not an afterthought. He is to protect and lead his wife with gentleness loving her and allowing her to speak into every situation before he makes a decision. Wives look to your husbands for leadership just as you would the Lord. God will speak through your husband just as God speaks through the pastor. If the husband refuses to follow God, there is no hesitation for God to speak and lead the wife. But until the man refuses to step up, wives are to defer to their husbands. This is not a negative position for woman, but a place of honor. Wife even if you don't agree with the choice your husband makes, I urge you to respect your husband's power to lead. He will answer to God for making wrong choices, but remember this, **Romans 8:28 And we know that in all things God works for the good of those who love him, who have been called according to his purpose..**

Both husband and wife are to follow the Divine Structure set forth in the Word of God. This is the "heart" of our struggle learning to follow God's structure forsaking selfish desires. Too often I see husbands, wives, even children striving to gain selfish control in the family structure thinking their ideals and desires are better than everyone else, even better suited making more sense than Biblical truth. We make personal desire more important than Biblical truth proclaiming the Biblical standard too hard pushing forward in the works of our hands than having the audacity to blame God for our failures. When will we stop rebelling against the structure of God? When will we allow Him to lead us to a better and more fulfilled life? Ignoring biblical structure leads to bitterness surrounded with walls of self-induced righteousness, always finding fault in others to build our self-esteem…. What a pitiful sight!

Husbands honor and respect your wives as you would your own bodies. Listen, I do my best to treat Freda as my Queen. I am able to get out of bed before her most mornings putting on the coffee, making her breakfast, and serving her as she sits in her recliner. We then sit down to enjoy breakfast and biblical discussions on the studies of the day. These mornings set the mood for the day ahead. We pray over each other openly reassuring each other of our shared love, not just for ourselves but for God. I give her a place of prominence in everything I do. I always want her to ride with me, minster with me, buy groceries with me, or go visiting with me. I want to spend time with her every day going out to eat or cooking meals together. I am more than willing to sacrifice my selfish desires to spend time with her, making her feel important and needed and she is!

Love your wives as Christ loved the Church. Wow! That is a tall order no question about it husbands you are called to make the necessary sacrifices for your wife and family. This is such a foreign concept for most men today, but in order to provide peace and security for your wife you must be willing to sacrifice selfish desires to prove over and over again your love and devotion, not only to your wife but to your children as well. Husbands must be willing to sacrifice themselves for their wives as Christ sacrificed himself for the Church. When you love your wife in this way, she will pour respect and honor on you over and over. She will be more than willing to follow your leadership.

Ladies, learning to respect your husbands is such an important process for developing a healthy marriage. In this age of independence and defiance women are not willing to respect men worthy of such. This leads women into the trap of spiritual poverty, leading them into a vicious cycle of jumping from one relationship to another searching for completeness and fulfillment. This is the product of not knowing or misunderstanding biblical structure. Be faithful to dig into the Word of God gaining knowledge and understanding, releasing the power of God into your life.

More is said about the husband loving and honoring his wife. Man carries the weight of responsibility for protection and harmony. This leads me to talk about the need to leave your father and mother, taking your wife and starting your new family. Allowing parents to interfere in your marriage will lead to slander and heartache. This is really important; never speak ill of your mate in front of your parents unless you are eager for discord.

Robert and Kim's Story
A Testimony of Grace
Lesson Nine

I have grown increasingly concerned over marriages unwilling to compromise for one reason or another, each party steadfast and unwilling to give an inch, or feeling entitled to more without giving more. I am concerned about the young man feeling trapped needing to get away for personal time with his friend or hobbies while the young woman left at home feeling neglected longing for personal time with their husbands to fulfill their emotional needs. With children these feelings only intensify. How sad to see so many husbands and wives unwilling to find common ground moving quickly into divorce thinking they have found an escape from there sadness. I see far too many young women looking, in all the wrong places, for the wrong reasons ending up in relationships with very little happiness and too much anger leaving her to asking this question, "Is there any hope for me? Will I ever find the right man?"

This chapter is delivered from two perspectives: the viewpoint of the wife (Kim) and the viewpoint of the husband (Robert). The purpose of this format is to engage each perspective, helping both the husband and wife to find and understand the path to restoration not separation. It is imperative for you to feel the frustration and pain each member of this marriage suffered as well as seeing how God directed their paths back into each other's arms. The importance of communication and forgiveness is high-lighted in this section.

PART I: Drifting Apart!

(Kim)
As a young girl I found myself in a relationship at 14, pregnant at 17 and married. I bet you can already guess how all this turned out? Well, you may be surprised to find out I have been married to the same wonderful man (Robert) for 28 years. I was in love and had the world by the tail. Life was going to be wonderful. When you're a child you think like a child, never thinking things through, and never able to account for the coming hardships of life. You try to convince yourself everything is going to be all right, but when your world begins to fall apart you realize just how unprepared you are. I went from being a junior in high school to dropping out due to problems with my pregnancy, to getting married. Having our first baby within a nine month period didn't allow me to think

at all about the problems I would soon face. It was like being in a race and I was gasping for air, trying to catch up with everybody else. My baby became the focus of my life so I set up housekeeping, raising my baby girl, and trying to take care of my husband. So life rolled on for two years and I had our second child, this time a baby boy. Life consisted of potty training one child, raising another baby, taking care of the house, and trying to take care of my husband, you talk about monotony? Nonetheless I trudged on, all the more determined to make it work. I felt trapped, no adult to share my thoughts or struggles with and when Robert came home well....

(Robert)
As the man of the house I thought my duties consisted of working hard making enough money to house and feed my family. With my responsibilities having been met, I would come home find my recliner and entered into my rest. It was my reward for being a good husband, or so I thought. The call of a husband is to work hard providing for his family which I did, but there is more than just being a provider. Right up front I want you, the reader, to know that I carry the weight of abusing my wife by ignoring her needs for many years. I have learned that the man is responsible for the spiritual and emotional needs of his family as well as the financial. Men it takes courage and strength to come home after a hard day of labor and still find the time to show your family the grace of God. My failure early on was not helping Kim at home. Kim did it all from writing out the bills, to cooking, cleaning, changing diapers, and even bringing me my dinner to my recliner! I loved Kim with all my heart but I didn't know a thing about loving her as Christ loved the Church.
(Kim)

Being a mother was my life. Seeing my children growing up and learning kept me motivated. When my son was old enough to play T-ball I was his coach. I would do anything I could for my children. The best I remember, Robert and I never raised our voices at each other probably because we were lost in two separate worlds his at work and mine with the kids. Ignoring each made for a strange sense of peace. But this peace did not satisfy. I never took time to think about what my needs, let alone having my needs met. I was so focus on my children that I not only lost sight of my needs but I lost sight of God. I was letting Robert off the hook at home in exchange for this strange sense of peace. Neither of us was staying in the Word of God, thus a huge void was being created in our lives. We were lost in our own separate worlds. As our children got older, they began to help out around the house making the load on my shoulders lighter, allowing me time to find a job and start working outside the home. I had a connection with other adults, a place for social interaction. I never expected Robert to meet my emotional needs, but now I see this as a huge mistake.

(Robert)
I thought we had a perfect marriage. I had two kids I loved dearly, I was earning enough money to live on and on top of that I had a beautiful wife... what else was there? WOW, was I blind? I never noticed the emptiness in Kim's eyes or cry for attention from the man of her dreams. We drifted apart with our jobs providing the social interaction in the absence of each other's attention. While jobs and raising children are important without God, what do they profit you? Value is found in a relationship with God, not your children, and certainly not in your job. There was a time fast approaching

that Kim and I would have to meet our struggles head on or lose each other in the sea of neglect.

(Kim)

After being Robert's wife for twenty years, and my son having just finished High School I felt all alone. My life had revolved around my children and now they were gone. I felt lost and unfulfilled. I had no purpose! I never had talked to Robert about my feelings and now that I needed him to listen, I didn't know what to say. I was intimidated by Robert as he talked over me. I was lost in the ocean of my futility. I lost my ability to express my inner most needs, but I learned something. I was no longer deceived into thinking I had a perfect marriage. Grace from God inters into us completing God's design for mankind and surprises with harsh reality to bring us to a place of change. I so needed to be touched and filled with the grace of God. I could not see myself as valuable to God, nor did I see the value of God in me or in my family. Two years of being empty nesters, mounting financial problems, and not being able to tell Robert how bad the finances were resulted in Robert blowing up at me for the first time. I was about to explode unable to find my way out of the darkness I turned to a new direction. I was unable to talk to Robert so I started going out to find release from the feelings of emptiness. This was the start of a search for meaning, fulfillment, and happiness but I was going the wrong way.

(Robert)

Yes, I blew up at her. I never talked to Kim about our finances so I thought everything was okay. I could not understand how we could make so much money and be facing bankruptcy. I was angry at Kim, myself, everything and everybody. How does a man not know the finances of his family? God ordained us as leaders of the family, even being bad with money I should have sit down with Kim and helped with the finances. Instead I left her all alone to deal with the impending doom. This is where men of God should stand up and know the perils facing their family. Adam failed to take a stand against the enemy in the Garden and it seems like ever since men have a hard time standing for what's right. I rolled over Kim like a steam roller. The fear and frustration of my heart ignored what was happening inside of her.

(Kim)
At this point with my voice silenced, my heart empty, and my emotions drained I moved out. I was hoping to be able to sort things out finding clarity and purpose. I moved in with a friend I knew from work. She had been divorced three times this was the only option that made sense at the time. Satan is like a roaring lion seeking to devour me; I was next on his dinner menu. His deception blinded me from the truth, and I headed into the abyss of darkness. When seeking counsel do not run to the world but to men and women who know God and will tell you the truth no matters how much it might hurt! I had not moved out with the intentions of leaving him, just sorting things out. That was my first mistake. My second mistake was going out with my new roommate to forget the problems I had ran from. My new roommate introduced me to a male friend of hers... Another mistake, one thing led to another and I had an affair. Running from my problems into the arms of another man was not the right solution. Until my heart changed I could not expect anything different, no matter how many different or new relationships I sought. Without God healing is not complete.

(Robert)

Kim left and I thought our marriage was over. I was devastated. I could not stay in the house, so I moved into an apartment close to my work and I began a search of my own. My search began with God, not that I was better than Kim, but I was desperate. I had nowhere else to turn. I needed divine intervention. When God speaks and you listen to His voice, you begin to see things you should have been doing all along. It becomes crystal clear. I felt so guilty for neglecting my wife. In my desperation, I was willing to anything to bring my wife back home. Why do we wait until all is lost to turn to God? I became a praying fool. I listened to Christian music, read everything I could set my eyes upon. I made many trips to the book store looking for anything related to Godly marriages. I read and I waited. For three months I prayed and searched for God, all the while learning to look past Kim. I realized I needed to get right with God first! I could not help her if I wasn't right with God. One day on my way to church missing the love of my life, I felt so unloved so I began praying earnestly wanting to feel loved... Just before reaching church, I heard God whispered, "Robert I love you." As those words sunk deep into my soul, I was overwhelmed with the love of God. I melted into an ocean of joyful tears. I knew God was listening to me I knew God was in control. What followed was peace, peace beyond explanation. I knew then that I could wait until it snowed in Texas in the middle of July for Kim to come home. God was with me healing me, and leading me, into forgiveness; not just forgiving Kim, but forgiving myself for neglecting my wife.

PART II: Finding the Grace to Forgive!

(Kim)

In spite of my actions, I still loved Robert. After spending three months separated from him I went home hoping. I wanted our marriage to work, but darkness still clouded my heart. I was still mixed up and empty. As long as sin reigns, your emotions are confused flip-flopping back and forth. Your ability to think clearly is obstructed by the darkness of unforgiven sin. The darkness hides the truth. At this point the truth just sounded stupid. As long as you rebel against the truth trying to hide your sin, there can be no enlightenment. You see, I thought if I told Robert the truth he would leave me and I would be all alone... so I didn't. This was the problem in the first place, not speaking up, hiding hoping all of this mess would just go away. When the scripture talks about the roaring lion waiting to devour you, I know the meaning. Guilt was consuming me, eating me one bite at a time. Slowly I was being overtaken by the power of darkness. I could not stop the slow yet steady advances. I started going to church with Robert and I wanted to find God, but the harder I tried all the more Satan whispered His deceit into my ears... How will I ever get out of the mess!

(Robert)
Kim was home and I was happy but things where still not right. I knew something was wrong; she was so secretive. From bolted doors, to hiding her phone and not letting me see her computer - I just didn't understand. One day I found her Myspace page. I confronted her about all the people I didn't know. Peering into her secrets made her run away again. Right back to the same friend she had stayed with before. Once again I was crushed. I cried out, "Lord, help me to understand what is going on!" My prayers became fervent I wanted my wife back. God was still working. He was moving over me, keeping me strong in the midst of my storm. Another three months

went by one Saturday night she called me and asked me to come over for coffee. I took a book by Joyce Myers with me, **"Battlefield of the Mind,"** I asked her to read it and she did. That next weekend she moved back in with me.

(Kim)

I so wanted to be able to love Robert with all my heart. I came home the second time on October 8th our anniversary. Shortly after that we renewed our vows in front of our family. I was hoping that the darkness had come to an end. There was only one way out of the darkness and it began with the truth. As long as I hid the truth, Satan had a rope, a connection, a grip that drug me back to the darkness at my weakest moments. The chains that hold you captive can only be broken by the Truth. Robert and I were attending a church, getting involved and the darkness seemed to be in the past. For two years I lived in the shadows of darkness, not yet surrendered to the Light. I was still broken, still having unresolved issues hanging over my head. You can live on the edge of darkness just so long until you feel the tug of that evil connection growing stronger and stronger... until you give in.

(Robert)

It had been two years! I thought everything was ok! We are going to church. We both loved the church and felt like we belonged... I thought we were on the mend. Suddenly I was blindsided, feeling like a load of bricks had just fallen on me, crushing and robbing me of my hope. Just because things look good on the outside does not mean all is good on the inside. It takes more than just going to church to make things right. If a person does not submit to the truth any perceived change will be short lived! Kim left again on a Friday and that night I was filled with anguish, brokenhearted and drained of all strength. My hope was fading fast. I was so confused. Everything had seemed so much better. Restoration cannot be realized without both husband and wife bringing everything into the light. The only hope we had was the truth!

(Kim)
I needed to tell Robert why I left or at least give him something that might make sense. I was going to meet with him Saturday evening but came down with a nasty migraine and could not drive. We changed our meeting to Sunday. I didn't know it but, God was at work. I knew what had to be done, I was going to tell Robert everything but God was putting all the pieces together setting Robert and myself up to step into His will.

(Robert)
Looking back I am so grateful for Kim not coming Saturday. It gave God time to work on my attitude. Saturday, my anguish had turned to anger and I was done with my marriage, but God was in control not allowing me to see Kim until He had brought me to a place of forgiveness. At this point I did not know why Kim kept leaving me. I just knew I had, had enough. God gave me time to let all the anger and hurt out and, believe me! I spewed, simmered, and boiled over with anger. Sunday morning I was hung over with hurt and anger. My mind was filled with thoughts of divorce. I just couldn't bring myself to go to church. So I went out on the patio and prayed. When things seem hopeless, God is still able to deliver the goods. He is faithful to give us what we need." I prayed, and deep within me God revealed a truth I needed to hear... God whispered, "Kim had an affair." I prayed, "Dear God, what do I do now?" God said, "Love her, forgive her, and lead her back to me." God

revealed the torment of her guilt and my anger melted away. I had to see beyond my hurt. I had to see the heart of God, and when I did He let me see Kim's heart. My soul groaned with compassion for her. Sunday when Kim arrived at the house, I opened the door, opened my arms, and we hugged. I will never forget that moment Kim squeezed me harder than ever; we just held each other. Kim was weighed down with guilt. I could clearly see it now. I believe she was just a hair shy of it all being more than she could handle.

(Kim)

After we hugged, Robert sat down and I knelt in front of him and before I could start he said, "I know why you have been running." Those words cracked the dam. Trying to hold my emotions back, they came rushing out in trembling waves of tears. Robert wrapped his arms around me and whispered into my ear, "I am going to help you through this." I got hold of myself and began to tell him about the affairs. Telling just part of the truth doesn't set you free, only the whole truth does. It takes the whole truth for God to complete His work in you. I was still feeling the tug of Satan trying to stop me from telling the whole truth. I was still weak, desperately seeking the truth and battling my fleshly feelings that eventually overwhelmed me. I figured two of the affairs were all I could confess for fear of losing Robert. I was having the hardest time letting go and trusting God.

(Robert)

I still can't believe how calm I was! Kim told me about the affairs and all I could think of was helping her. My heart was full of compassion for her, but in the back of mind I was still getting a divorce. It was a shield protecting me from the hurt.

God has a way of working things out, even if we have our minds made to go another way. Never underestimate the knowledge and power of God! For the next week we talked and cried, trying to find a way past the hurt, loneliness, neglect, and emptiness. At the end of the week, I found two hidden emails to two different men. I didn't open them afraid of what I might find, so I asked Kim about them. Openness is essential for restoration no hidden texts, social media pages, E-mails or such. When it comes to your spouse your life should be an open book.

(Kim)
I wanted to run, but God was not finished and I still was hiding darkness within, not trusting God or Robert with the whole truth. So when Robert confronted me with the two emails I thought all was lost... but it was all or nothing. I had no other choice. God had put me right where He wanted me surrendering, to Him and to Robert. I confessed the final affair and finally the whole truth was out. I was afraid of what Robert was going to do or say. Fear is powerful, but we should never let it close the door on love.

(Robert)
The news of the final affair sunk me into the sea of despair. I didn't know it, but God had us both right where He wanted. With the whole truth on the table, I was humbled by the weight of this news. It all became so clear. The neglect I inflicted upon her cause me to crumble with guilt. Truly God had set a divine appointment. God was ready to do his miracle in each of our hearts. God whispered into my soul, "Show Kim My grace and love." I never felt so unsure or out of control as I

did at that moment. I didn't have a clue as to what I should do - I was numb. We talked an hour or so and then I felt God moving us to take a walk. There are times you need to sit still and wait for God to direct your path. Our problem is rushing through what we think instead of waiting for God to lead. We walked across the street to the park and there in the park was a walking path. I looked down at the path and right there in front of me it said, "Start Here." God must have a sense of humor suddenly it was all too easy. I turned to Kim and said, "Today is a new day and we are going to have a fresh start." My mind screamed silently, WHAT! I realized that God had put those words in heart to say. God couldn't be any clearer - I was not allowed to leave Kim. Forgiveness flooded my heart as it was transferred over to her. The work of God was being accomplished much like that of Hosea of the Old Testament. The responsibility for restoration as well as divine reconciliation rests upon the husband. Then and only then can a marriage become what God intended.

(Kim)
I heard the words Robert spoke, but I couldn't bring myself to believe it possible that could Robert forgive me. How! I can't even forgive myself! We walked and talked along the path coming upon a small bridge over a creek... we stopped. Robert turned and took my hands looking straight into my eyes said, "When we walk over this bridge we are leaving everything behind, we will be starting a new life together." We turned and walked hand in hand across the bridge to the other side turned to each other with tears streaming down our cheeks embraced and hugged. Robert whispered in my ear, "I forgive you, I love you." Having the grace of God wash over you at the lowest point of your life is beyond words, but I felt the cleanest, most

refreshing, euphoric feeling ever. It was the grace of God! God had just set me free. Free from guilt, free from Satan's hold on me, free to love Robert with all my heart, I could breathe again.

(Robert)
Crossing that bridge with Kim was a God thing He kept speaking directly into my heart. As we hugged I could feel the grace of God flowing, I could feel the transformation taking place in Kim. God breathed into me saying, "I have forgiven you. If you want your marriage to work, you have to give grace to Kim." The thoughts of divorce vanished as I gave Kim the grace that God had given me. I wanted my marriage... I loved Kim way too much to let her go. God's love overcomes all obstacles, cleanses from all sin, frees us from any hurt, and gives us a new heart - one that pursues God. My strength was rooted in the sacrifice Jesus made for me. I could see Jesus on the cross suffering for me and if He was willing to suffer for my salvation then I would suffer to keep Kim in my life. Too many people are quick to forsake their marriage. No matter how you feel God hates divorce. Love is worthy of your suffering through hardship and all along seeking God's direction and not your own. Stop trying to find an easy way out and learn to trust God and stick it out. God can bring His healing touch to your marriage. I know firsthand that there is no hurt so great that God cannot mend... Praise God!

I felt so free! I cannot imagine anything being better than the feeling of being set free from sin's grasp. Yes, this was more that finding my way back to Robert it was me finding my way to God. It has been one years since that walk across the bridge and with each passing day Robert and I fall more and more in love. The past seems like a nightmare a vague memory from a distant time. There is nothing beyond the grace of God.

Nothing so separates you from God that He cannot reach out and gather you up in His arms, if you let Him. While in the midst of your struggle it's hard to see clearly, just wait, He will show you the way out grace comes to those who are willing to wait on God. There is no problem that the grace of God will not fix. You have a choice you can trust God to restore your marriage or you can run from your divine appointment with God. If you're willing God is ready to pour grace and forgiveness into your marriage.

(Kim)

I felt so free! I cannot imagine anything being better than the feeling of being set free from sin's grasp. Yes, this was more than finding my way back to Robert. It was me finding my way back to God. It has been four years since that walk across the bridge and with each passing day Robert and I fall more in love. The past seems like a nightmare, a vague memory from a distant time. There is nothing beyond the grace of God. Nothing can separate you from God that He cannot reach out gathering you in His arms if you let Him. While in the midst of your struggle, it is hard to see clearly. Just wait, He will show you the way out. Grace comes to those who are willing to wait on God. There is no problem that the grace of God will not fix. You have a choice; you can trust God to restore your marriage, or you can run from your divine appointment. I you're willing, god is ready to pour grace and forgiveness into your marriage.

What a wonderful testimony of enduring grace. To this very day Robert and Kim are happily married and reaching out to other married couples, giving them guidance and hope for enduring the hardships of marriage. Glory to God!

IN LIKE MANNER
Lesson Ten

Genesis 2:21-25 "**And the Lord God caused a deep sleep to fall upon Adam; and while he slept, He took one of his ribs or a part of his side and closed up the [place with] flesh. And the rib or part of his side which the Lord God had taken from the man He built up and made into a woman, and He brought her to the man. Then Adam said, "This [creature] is now bone of my bones and flesh of my flesh;" she shall be called Woman, because she was taken out of a man. Therefore a man shall leave his father and his mother and shall become united and cleave to his wife, and they shall become one flesh. And the man and his wife were both naked and were not embarrassed or ashamed in each other's presence."**

To find out the true intention of God's purpose, you must go to the first place it is mentioned, and there you will find the pure, undefiled reason behind the principle. In the passage above we find the first mention of marriage and what God designed for a man and women. This one passage transcends time and can solve a myriad of moral and social ills. Without a doubt we know that God intended marriage to be between a man and a woman, and that marriage was meant to last a lifetime. Later in **Deuteronomy 24,** Moses' law makes a provision for divorce. There we find the provision for this divorce decree was directed at the request of the hard hearted men desiring a way to divorce their wives, funny how men can desire such rules that do not apply to them. In the **Matthew 19,** Jesus replies with these words, "but it was not that way from the beginning," referring back to **Genesis 2**.

Jesus does make a concession in this matter allowing the Moses decree to stand, restating divorce is not acceptable except in the case of sexual immorality. Grace is given to those victims of adultery, yet in the scripture I see a higher calling. The intention of the original text concerning marriage teaches us that marriage is meant to last a lifetime. Grace is not for running but staying! Don't be so quick to run out of marriage claiming exemptions. Grace prompt's you to reach out to your spouse bringing them back into the love of God. Once married we become responsible for each other helping each other remain in the grace of God. I have been criticized for this belief, but when I turn to **I Peter 3,** a segment is written to both the wife and the husband. Each segment begins with these words, "In like manner." To get the full meaning of this passage, we have to go back to chapter two and read to get the correct understanding of, "In like manner."

I Peter 2: 19; Now, it is commendable if, because of one's understanding of God, someone should endure pain through suffering unjustly. 20 But what praise comes from enduring patiently when you have sinned and are beaten for it? But if you endure steadfastly when you've done the righteous thing and suffer for it, this is commendable before God. 21 You were called to this kind of endurance, because Christ suffered on your behalf. He left you an example so that you might follow in his footsteps.

I Peter 3:1 & 7; Wives, likewise, submit to your own husbands. Do this so that even if some of them refuse to believe the word, they may be won without a word by

their wives' way of life. 7 Husbands, likewise, submit by living with your wife in ways that honor her, knowing that she is the weaker partner. Honor her all the more, as she is also a coheir of the gracious care of life. Do this so that your prayers won't be hindered.

While enduring Marriage or family hardships you are still called to function as an obedient servant. This obedience to God's plan brings Heavenly favor into your life. I conclude that both husband and wife are called to endure hardship for the sake of finding favor with God. Even in the event of sexual immorality we should seek restoration, not quickly running away seeking a divorce, but rather endure letting the grace of God have its perfect work. This is where the grace of God empowers and leads us through the deep waters of marital struggles. God's design is not divorce but reconciliation! I am so glad God sought not to divorce the human race, but rather endures our adultery seeking to reconcile all who will listen to His call. Your marriage and the sanctity of your family is worth fighting for, warring against the fiery darts keeping the family structure united and safe yielding physical and spiritual fruit. Remember the enemy is not your spouse or your kids, but the works of Satan. Don't let Him split or destroy the most important institution intended for the teaching of salvation building a spiritual legacy. I don't hear many talking about the power of the family unit in building the Kingdom of God, but I do not see a better vehicle for the reconciliation of society than the family. The failure of the family structure dictates the moral decline of society. Failure to maintain Biblical principles for family and Church is rapidly turning us into a Godless society.

God sees the institution of marriage, the husband and wife relationship, as a reflection of our love for Him. Listed below with brief commentary are just a few of the scriptures speaking to God's perspective on marriage.

Proverbs 5:18-19 "May your fountain be blessed, and may you rejoice in the wife of your youth. A loving doe, a graceful deer-- may her breasts satisfy you always, may you ever be captivated by her love."

God has designed men to pursue the structure of family it is a part of man's purpose adding to their since of fulfillment. A Godly woman is to be treasured for she will become a fountain of blessings as she loves and supports man in the institution of marriage. When man honors his wife as his equal and the object of his affection marriage takes on a much deeper meaning. For any husband the greatest joys of life are rooted in his wife when she returns his honor and affection with sincere love and respect. Listen nothing titillates or motivates a man more than a Godly woman.

Proverbs 12:4 "A wife of noble character is her husband's crown, but a disgraceful wife is like decay in his bones."

The wife can also represent the universal bride of Christ. Her noble character brings Glory to God and her husband. Many are the times people praise me for having such a precious and noble wife such as Freda. Many are the blessings God pours through her into my life and the most amazing thing is that she doesn't notice just how wonderful she is nor does she know how thankful and blessed I am to have such a wonderful wife. On the other hand the woman who is disgraceful, demanding, loud, and selfish brings great reproach not only on God His kingdom but on her husband. A woman can be a blessing or a curse. The choice between the two will rest in her willingness to take her place or rebel against God's structure.

Proverbs 31:10 "A wife of noble character is worth far more than rubies, who can find?"

A wife who desires the structure of God accepting her position before God and her husband is half of the formula bringing unity into the marriage. Following Biblical structure is essential to a healthy union. A good question to ask yourself is, "Why is following the Biblical structure so hard? " The answer might be your unwillingness to accept Biblical structure. Sometimes we get things turned upside down. Ladies, don't be afraid of words such as "submit" or "proper place." These words do not bind but set you free. They do not place you under or beneath him, but simple means he is your protector or covering against the this present world. We do not need to reinvent the process the Creator has given. His plan is the perfect plan.

Proverbs 20:6-7 "Many a man claims to have unfailing love, but a faithful man who can find? The righteous man leads a blameless life; blessed are his children after him." Stop deceiving yourself with a poverty mentality depriving your family of the necessary parts of your life to lead your family into a relationship with Christ. Be a faithful husband to your wife. Be a faithful father to your children teaching them the ways of God. Be a consistent example demonstrating Godly behavior and be a righteous man building a spiritual heritage that will be passed on to your children. Stop selling yourself short. Stop those feelings of inadequacy. Stop thinking small, and stop letting yourself get stuck in weakness ignoring the strength of God within.

Marriage after Divorce?

Lesson Eleven

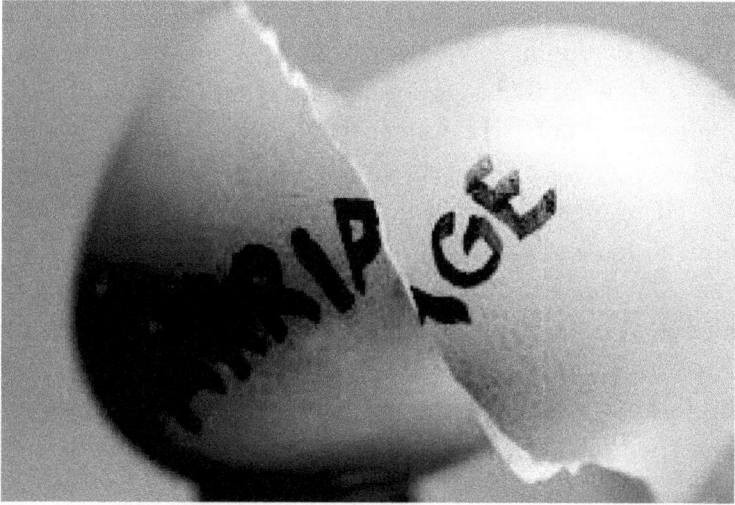

Paul makes know in Romans 7, that sin is always going to be a struggle while we are in the flesh. A war between mind and heart tears at our very souls; Satan on one hand seeking to strip us of our heavenly treasure, and on the other the Spirit of God seeking to lead us deeper into biblical truth establishing each of us upon heaven's foundation. God hates all sin and especially divorce, but He gives grace to the repentant sinner, Praise God! The choice is yours to make chose the fleshly desires and remain in bondage to earthly thinking or seek Jesus and the Truth of the Bible and be set free. This lesson centers its attention on what the Bible says about grace in our marriages.

DON'T ABUSE GRACE
What then? Shall we sin because we are not under law but under grace?

"My way or the highway, I am what I am, I cannot change. I don't care what God says, I am doing what I want. I have to change things before I can come to God. I am stuck in this mess with no way out!" These statements among others have been uttered by people during my two years here in Columbus Ohio, all have a common theme, "I am settling for less than what God desires to give." Failure has become such a part of their lives they are left with nothing more than excuses to keep from dealing with personal weakness, becoming comfortable with less keeps people form seeing the power of God. Their failure is failing to enact the measure of faith they have. Faith in God would deliver them, but instead they have chosen to be rooted in the desires of their flesh. Selfish desires captivate people in earthly wisdom leading them away from divine truth while thinking they are justified in their sin.

God has a better plan for your life! Rebuke the Word of God all you want! Elevate the sensual desires of your flesh as oft as you will, but nothing allows you to live in the freedom as does the plan of God. HIS plan not only saves your soul by placing your faith solely in Jesus, but provides you hope of a brighter and ultimately glorious future. It does not mean all struggles cease, but that HIS plan will lead you and empower you through your struggles. And while waiting for our future we live presently in the love of our Heavenly Father that produces peace in any of our circumstances. There are so many times HIS grace leaves me speechless. Trusting in Jesus is not a pot luck dinner picking and choosing what you like. Often we look at the Word of God like a picky eater at the dinner table demanding only deserts. Trusting God is trusting in the whole plan whether portions of it suit you or not. If we chose to reject God's plan we forfeit HIS freedom, from the chains of earthly wisdom. You select earthly or fleshly wisdom over Godly wisdom thinking you have found freedom but actually you have imprisoned yourself in the darkness of sin leading you to eternal condemnation. When you elevate your fleshly desires above the plan of God you are rejecting God, rejecting HIS freedom, and rejecting the eternal joy of heaven.

There are three building blocks that provide us freedom from sin and its eternal demise: Faith, Hope and Love.

Faith in God, not personal desires, yields Salvation "For by grace you are saved through faith in Jesus Christ." Again Paul in the book of Romans tells us we are sinners and all have fallen short of God's standard. God loved us even as sinners and wants to fulfill HIS plan of salvation in each of our hearts. If we believe Jesus robed in flesh died on the cross, shed HIS blood for the sins of mankind, was buried but rose again, you can be saved. This is where we come to grips with the plan of God moving from an earthly mindset into a heavenly way of thinking and loving. This plan is the only way to eternal salvation finding freedom from the ill effects of sin delivering us from the clutches of Hell into eternal glory as joint heirs with Jesus. If you have not received Jesus as your savior this is where you start. Before you can be reconciled with your spouse you must be reconciled to God. (**Romans 3:23, Romans 6:23, Romans 5:8, Romans 10:9-13**)

Hope is the inheritance of the children of God. We have a glorious future.

1 Thess. 4:13–18, Brothers and sisters, we do not want you to be uninformed about those who sleep in death, so that you do not grieve like the rest of mankind, who have no hope. 14 For we believe that Jesus died and rose again, and so we believe that God will bring with Jesus those who have fallen asleep in him. 15 According to the Lord's word, we tell you that we who are still alive, who are left until the coming of the Lord, will certainly not precede those who have fallen asleep. 16 For the Lord himself will come down from heaven, with a loud command, with the voice of the archangel and with the trumpet call of God, and the dead in Christ will rise first. 17 After that, we who are still alive and are left will be caught up together with them in the clouds to meet the Lord in the air. And so we will be with the Lorde forever. 18 Therefore encourage one another with these words.

Stress, fear, anger and doubts debilitate, robbing us of hope, clouding the cognitive process, and keeping us from taking proper action. The Hope of Jesus addresses each of these harmful qualities freeing us from the chains of earthly wisdom allowing us to act upon biblical principal. Relationships, marriages, families, and churches need something to hope in, a future with great possibilities. Not just Hope in eternal things yet to come, but of healing and reconciliation right here, right now! The closer you grow towards Jesus the less room there is for Satan to destroy your family. To me, this is the beauty of Hope, for increase hope all I have to do is seek more of Jesus.

Love is the attitude children of God are to live under. In fact, it is declared the greatest of these three virtues

I Cor. 13, If I speak in the tongues of men and of angels, but have not love, I am only a resounding gong or a clanging cymbal. 2 If I have the gift of prophecy and can fathom all mysteries and all knowledge, and if I have a faith that can move mountains, but have not love, I am nothing. 3 If I give all I possess to the poor and surrender my body to the flames, but have not love, I gain nothing. 4 Love is patient, love is kind. It does not envy, it does not boast, it is not proud. 5 It is not rude, it is not self-seeking, it is not easily angered, it keeps no record of wrongs. 6 Love does not delight in evil but rejoices with the truth. 7 It always protects, always trusts, always hopes, will always persevere. 8 Love never fails. But where there are prophecies, they will cease; where there are tongues, they will be stilled; where there is knowledge, it will pass away. 9 For we know in part and we prophesy in part, 10 but when perfection comes, the imperfect disappears. 11 When I was a child, I talked like a child I thought like a child, I reasoned like a child. When I became a man, I put childish ways behind me. 12 Now we see but a poor reflection as in a mirror; then we shall see face to face. Now I know in part; then I shall know fully, even as I am fully known. 13 And now these three remain: faith, hope and love. But the greatest of these is love.

The more you learn about your Hope in Jesus the more you're going to realize how much He loves you! You will also learn that the power of His love experienced here on earth is but a reflection of the love you will experience in heaven. You see, your marriage, family, and even Church life is meant to be a reflection of our relationship with God. If we search out the Word and apply the biblical principles set forth, we learn all the more the power of God's love in our hearts minds and lives. As we grow in love with God, we cannot help but grow more in love with our families. But it does not stop there. We also grow stronger in grace, stronger in our understanding of God's Word, and stronger in divine or heavenly wisdom. Be serious students of the Word!!

When Divorce Happens

Let me say this one more time. I believe God hates divorce and as Christians we should do everything in our power to keep our marriages alive, even if it means enduring hardship, unfaithfulness, or falling out of love with your spouse. I would contend that there are scriptural grounds for divorce that covers adultery, but Jesus was quick to add, "But it was not that way in the beginning!" Paul speaks concerning a believer married to an unbeliever where the unbeliever leaves (meaning abandonment) resulting in the believer not being responsible to save the marriage.

1 Corinthians 7:15-16, but if a spouse who doesn't believe chooses to leave, then let them leave. The brother or sister isn't tied down in these circumstances. God has called you to peace. 16 How do you know as a wife if you will save your husband? Or how do you know as a husband if you will save your wife?

I would also want to say this, divorce and remarriage before your salvation should not to be held against you. To do so, in my opinion, is to limit the effect of grace and forgiveness. For example to hold a man's past prior to his salvation against him when seeking the position of pastor the use of "husband of one wife," culturally is not speaking to divorce but the practice of polygamy. Even if you don't agree with me on this how can we hold a person responsible for a law or concept meant for Christians and not sinners. **II Corinthians 5:17** is very clear, **"Therefore if anyone is in Christ, he is a new creature; the old things passed away; behold, new things have come."** Or how about **Isaiah 43:18-19, "Forget the former things; do not dwell on the past. 19 See, I am doing a new thing! Now it springs up; do you not perceive it? I am making a way in the wilderness and streams in the wasteland."**

The culture has always made allowances for divorce as in **Deut. 24:1-4.** Even though God has always had a better plan, nothing illustrates the need for grace better than marriage. In fact, I believe that God has used marriage and family to help teach us how our Heavenly Father seeks to love us, to correct us, lead us, but most of all how grace works within. Throughout the Bible, God speaks of the adultery of His people, the most familiar being that of Hosea and Gomer in the Old Testament **Hosea 1-3** and how Christ loves the Church being the pattern of how husbands are to love their wives in the New Testament taken from **Ephesians 5:22-33**. I contend that the way a husband and wife love each other is but a reflection of their love for God. As ugly and sinful as divorce is don't forget that grace abounds all the more. **Romans 5:20, The Law came in so that the transgression would increase; but where sin increased, grace abounded all the more.**

Listen even in my marriage of forty plus years grace is a constant. I see a Christian divorce and then remarriage as a single act of adultery. Remember grace is not given just so you can do as you will thus taking for granted God's grace. Abusing grace is a sign of selfishness and more often than not lacking in true repentance. Please do not justify your divorce on the back of grace. To do so will place yourself in rebellion to God's plan.

When you have exhausted all resources to restore your marriage after seeking godly counsel and you still find yourself stepping into divorce know this...... Forgiveness is possible! But before you steam head long into another relationship, I strongly urge you to do a lot of introspection, unpack your emotional baggage, and above all set your heart and mind on Jesus. I see too many men and women go from one relationship to another while never unpacking the emotional baggage of their past, dragging personal problems to each new relationship. Take time to free yourself from your past and prepare your soul for the future, both here on earth and the kingdom to come. You do this by sitting still and letting God speak from the pages of the Bible directly into your life. Seeking a relationship with man or a woman is not the source of your happiness God is the only way to lasting joy-filled relationships. Freedom from your past is the ability to unpack the excess baggage of emotional trauma before entering another love relationship, failure to do so will more than likely spell defeat for any new relationship. Taking time with God is where you will find the amazing work of grace. Spending time with God will teach you how to forgive yourself and forget all the wrongs done to you.

Micah 7:18 "Who else is like YOU, pardoning iniquity, overlooking the sin of the few remaining for his inheritance? He doesn't hold on to his anger forever; he delights in faithful love. 19 He will once again have compassion on us; he will tread down our iniquities. You will hurl all our sins into the depths of the sea. 20 You will provide faithfulness to Jacob, faithful love to Abraham, as you swore to our ancestors a long time ago."

When I think of forgiveness I cannot help but think upon the wonderings of the children of Israel. From the miracles of the ten plagues, the crossing of the Red Sea, pillar of fire by night and column of smoke by day, manna and water in the dessert, on and on we could go, and still the people wander off into the grip of rebellion and idols. In spite of the lack of faithfulness, the faithful Husband waited for His bride to come running back into His arms, always forgiving.

When the time comes to remarry, it is vital for you and your future spouse to establish biblical principal as a pattern to build upon so when trouble comes you can preserve your marriage. Again let me remind you that God means for marriage to be a reflection of our walk with Him. This makes marriage the centerpiece, not only the family but the church as well. The only way to understand the plan of God is to get into the Word there you will find truths for living, power for overcoming, and hope knowing that God is walking with you through the struggles of recovery from divorce and future marriage.

Philippians 1:9-11 "This is my prayer: that your love might become even more and more rich with knowledge and all kinds of insight. 10 I pray this so that you will be

able to decide what really matters and so you will be sincere and blameless on the day of Christ. 11 I pray that you will then be filled with the fruit of righteousness, which comes from Jesus Christ, in order to give glory and praise to God."

Most people today go into a relationship emotionally and spiritually bankrupt, yet God wants us to increase in Biblical knowledge and spiritual insight so we can enter into relationships rich in heavenly wisdom. This is not achieved without sacrificing time and effort to dig into the Word. So many complain about how hard it is to study the Bible. Let me say this, the speed in which you fall asleep while reading the Bible is a reflection of your spiritual depth. Don't let fleshly weakness keep you from becoming rich in heavenly wisdom. Not only does this understanding affect our minds, but our hearts as well leading us to live righteous lives. What an advantage this would be for every marriage to enter into a lifelong relationship built upon heavenly wisdom and not earth wisdom.

Philippians 2:1-8 "Therefore, if there is any encouragement in Christ, any comfort in love, any sharing in the Spirit, any sympathy, 2 complete my joy by thinking the same way, having the same love, being united, and agreeing with each other. 3 Don't do anything for selfish purposes, but with humility think of others as better than yourselves. 4 Instead of each person watching out for their own good, watch out for what is better for others. 5 Adopt the attitude that was in Christ Jesus: 6 Though he was in the form of God, he did not consider being equal with God something to exploit. 7 But he emptied himself

by taking the form of a slave and by becoming like human beings. When he found himself in the form of a human, 8 he humbled himself by becoming obedient to the point of death, even death on a cross."

This passage of scripture speaks to relationships and how we are to follow Christ example. We are in a very selfish society and I find most relationship struggles are rooted in the love of self over our love for our spouses. One of the things Freda and I learned a long time ago was while on our way home to pray - clearing our minds of the stress of the work day and turning our focus upon each other. What a change this simple ideal brought into our relationship. We could sit down for dinner without self-induced stress over petty desires. We would help each other clean up the kitchen and then tend to the kids and settle in for some shared time. Christ gave His all for the Church and husbands are to make the greater sacrifice defending and securing his family in the presence of God. You want peace this is where you find it in serving the needs of your family.

II Timothy 3:16-17 "Every scripture is inspired by God and is useful for teaching, for showing mistakes, for correcting, and for training character, 17 so that the person who belongs to God can be equipped to do everything that is good."

The richness of the Word is rooted in the truth of God's voice echoing into our hearts, molding and making us into what He desires not according to the flesh but according to the Spirit of God. We are to surrender to the Word letting it speak and empower us pulling down earthly wisdom and replacing it with heavenly wisdom allowing us, to reap the blessing of God. Only when we follow God's plan can we know the peace and joy of God in our marriages.

Freda and I have been discussing marriage and how spouses feed off each other's weaknesses to feel justified giving in to their own weakness. For example a husband filled the demon of jealousy picks at perceived acts of compromise in his wife to justify his drinking. On the other hand the wife uses her husband battle with alcohol to justify seeking comfort in the advice of other men creating an endless cycle that captivates the couple until the marriage is destroyed. Stop trying to fix or blame your spouse and turn to God letting Him set your mind and heart straight. Each the husband and wife is responsible for the weakness within themselves and only a personal pursuit of God will yield victory in your lives.

Miracles Still Happen!
Jimmy and Tara Lee Fulkerson's Testimony
Lesson Twelve and Conclusion

In Tara's Words, "On January 5th, 2010, a miracle happened. What my husband and I tried to do for years, on our own and failed miserably, yet with one encounter with the living God took care of struggles in a matter of seconds. Literally! In one moment we lived in despair, our house was in shambles. Yet in the next the desire to use, and drink, imprisoned by the same old feelings of guilt, shame, anxiety, depression, doom and gloom, and destructive habits were gone and replaced with new Hope, new Grace, and a new Love. Mercy met us, leading the way for Jimmy and I to find forgiveness. We started a brand new life together, FREE from years of Meth addiction, drugs of various types, bad choices, alcohol, fighting, drama, negativity, wrong thoughts and immoral behavior, along with all the resulting consequences. We had to learn how to set boundaries for personal growth, our relationship as well as with our friends, which was weird at first. We had no clue of what it was supposed to look like...lol. We were terribly co-dependent and had no idea how to handle life without manipulating, lying, or throwing fits to get what we wanted. Crashing, falling apart, habitually behaving badly, running from one party to the next, consumed us. The search for drugs and alcohol was the focus of our lives. **I'm not lying!** Learning to live in Hope, in spite of how things looked like on the outside, was tough! But that is the beauty of our Hope in Jesus, it kept us focused motivated, always looking up to see Jesus sitting on the right hand of the Father. Jimmy and I might find ourselves going through tough times just like before, but sin no longer had its grip on us. We no longer had to fall apart. We no longer had to have a meltdown turning to our addiction for comfort. We no longer had to say or do regrettable things. We no longer had to suffer a lifestyle of failure and its consequence. We had found healing in Jesus! We suddenly had GRACE to face the darkness of our past. We now had grace to face our daily struggles without falling apart.

I watched my husband transform before my very eyes! He turned into a man after God's own heart. Realization of God's love for us, even though we were all messed up was HUGE! Despite our mess, God loved us... and our love was fresh and alive. For the first time Jimmy and I were experiencing and receiving God's unconditional love.

The enemy meant to destroy us, but God used our struggle to build us up, making us stronger than ever. I thank Him for my marriage today. I thank God for my NEW life in Christ! I thank HIM for not giving up on us. Most of all I thank God for giving us HOPE in the midst of our darkness. I am a firm believer that God is good and He has made my life good and full of saving grace. Jimmy and I became a new creation in Christ and are committed to remaining faithful until the very end. There's no denying the redemption power of God His miracle has had a profound effect on our lives. What took us years, still not able to accomplish within ourselves, God accomplished in just one moment. We haven't drunk one drop of alcohol, or used since that day, and now here I am, five years later, still smiling about Saving Grace. NOW that's amazing! Nothing is impossible with Christ...Just saying!

There is Hope!

Isaiah 43:19 "For I am about to do something NEW! See, I have already begun! Do you not see it? I will make a pathway through the wilderness. I will create rivers in the dry wasteland."

Mr. Husband and Mrs. Wife one day you wake to find your family in chaos, your marriage on the brink of divorce, with anxious feelings leading to anger and frustration, opening the door to erroneous temptations outside the family structure. You may not like the sound of this, but the chaos within can only be stopped by seeking peace with God before you can give peace to anyone else. The root of your frustration lies within, not in your wife, not in your husband, and not in your children, but within YOU! If grace, forgiveness, and peace are to flow to your family, it has to flow through you. Husband! Wife! Set your life upon the foundation of Jesus Christ! With your needs met in Jesus you will be able to pour the necessary grace, forgiveness, and peace into your family creating harmony which is necessary for healing and restoration.

In the words of **Pastor Luis Burgos**, "I still believe in a God that can change anyone and a God that can do the miraculous through the willing. I still believe in a God who can redeem a city in an instant when his people surrender. I still believe in the impossible becoming possible with a God who specializes in doing the impossible. I still believe in the purpose he's placed on my life and the people around me. Through all the difficulty and hardship, by His grace, I have endured still believing."

The Creator of all things, YHWH, has given us every form and function needed for righteousness and life. Jehovah-Jireh has invested divine power, position, and privilege into every man and woman to bring forth fruit building not only family, but the Church enlarging the presence and influence of the Kingdom of God. I hope and pray we all are tapping into God's investment building his Kingdom bringing HIM great joy.

Men the commitment to your wife is but a reflection of your love for God. God instituted marriage as a reflection of our commitment, love, and faithfulness to God.

Ladies... Without making excuses, without rationalizing please realize this one very important principle. The way you trust in your husband is but a mirror of your trust in God. God instituted marriage as a reflection of our commitment to God on every level.

In **Jeremiah 3** we read;
"If a man divorces his wife and she leaves him and becomes another man's wife, he may not take her back again.

Doing that would utterly defile the land.

But you, Israel, have given yourself as a prostitute to many gods.

So what makes you think you can return to me?" says the Lord.

"Look up at the hilltops and consider this.

You have had sex with other gods on every one of them.

You waited for those gods like a thief lying in wait in the desert.

You defiled the land by your wicked prostitution to other gods.

That is why the rains have been withheld, and the spring rains have not come.

Yet in spite of this you are obstinate as a prostitute.

You refuse to be ashamed of what you have done.

Even now you say to me, 'You are my father!

You have been my faithful companion ever since I was young.

You will not always be angry with me, will you?

You will not be mad at me forever, will you?'

That is what you say, but you continually do all the evil that you can."

God desires absolute commitment just as a man and a woman are to commit to each other in marriage.

It took Freda and I a while to learn that life without hardships is a dream yet to be realized. Our past struggles have taught us to embrace the difficulties of our life expecting God to show up in a special way to deliver or empower us through troubled waters. I love resting in Jesus and letting HIM lead us through our darkness. Whether enduring arguments, financial problems, family issues, job issues, or Church headaches resting in Jesus is the only way to peace. We long to find a season without hardship but a last there is no joy without struggle just as there is no peace without Jesus... (**Psalm 37**)

One final word Mom, Dad do you teach your children the Word of God? Have you made time to pull the family together around a family altar of Biblical truth and prayer? Can I encourage you to do just that! See the value of family altars, family meals, family Bible reading, and family prayers as tools to lead your children into the family of God. Problems are solved and issues avoided with quality family time pointing each other to Jesus.

Deuteronomy 6:1-9 "Now these are the commandments, the regulations, and the case laws that the LORD your God commanded me to teach you to follow in the land you are entering to possess, 2 so that you will fear the LORD your God by keeping all his regulations and his commandments that I am commanding you—both you and your sons and daughters—all the days of your life and so that you will lengthen your life. 3 Listen to them, Israel! Follow them carefully so that things will go well for you and so that you will continue to multiply exactly as the LORD, your ancestors' God, promised you, in a land full of milk and honey. 4 Israel, listen! Our God is the LORD! Only the LORD! 5 Love the LORD your God with all your heart, all your being, and all your strength. 6 These words that I am commanding you today must always be on your minds. 7 Recite them to your children. Talk about them when you are sitting around your house and when you are out and about, when you are lying down and when you are getting up. 8 Tie them on your hand as a sign. They should

be on your forehead as a symbol. 9 Write them on your house's doorframes and on your city's gates."

BEING LIGHT, GIVING LOVE

Another book By Louis Nettleton

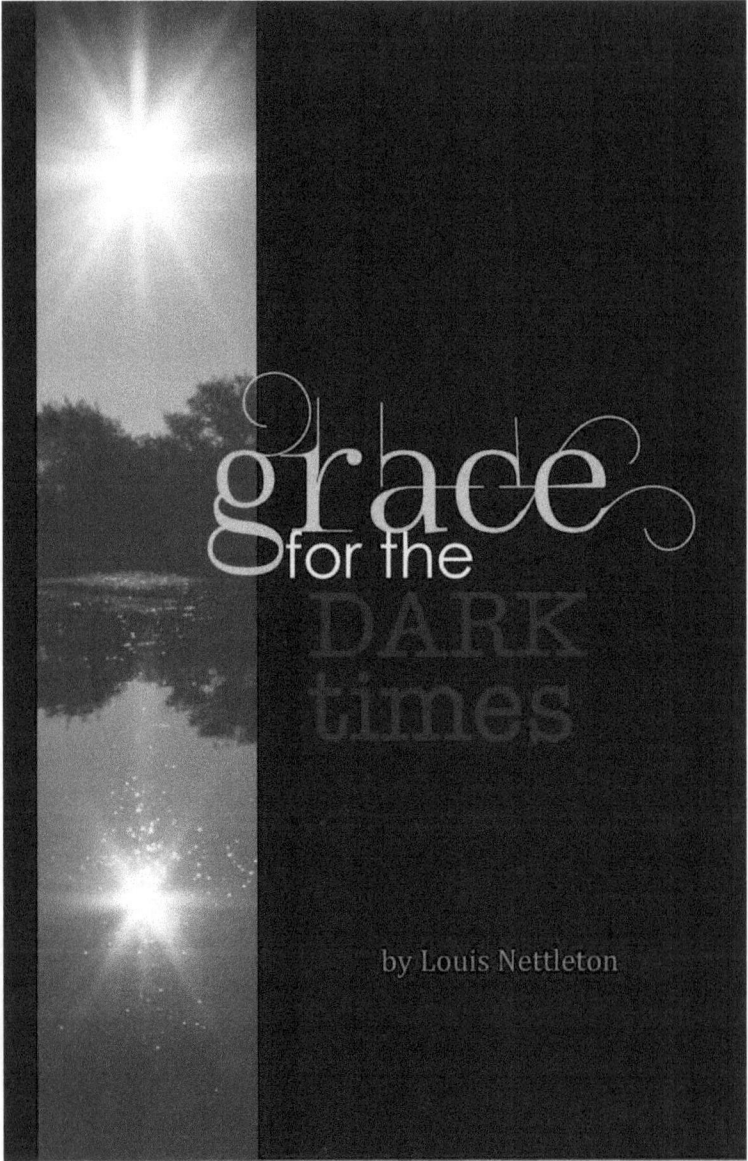

www.ingramcontent.com/pod-product-compliance
Lightning Source LLC
Chambersburg PA
CBHW060522030426
42337CB00015B/1972

* 9 7 8 1 9 4 0 6 0 9 5 2 2 *